The Book of Jonah

A SOCIAL JUSTICE COMMENTARY

The Book of Jonah
A SOCIAL JUSTICE COMMENTARY

Rabbi Dr. Shmuly Yanklowitz

Consulting Editors: Abraham J. Frost,
Suzanne Bring, and Judry Subar

with a foreword by
CHRISTINE HAYES, PhD

CENTRAL CONFERENCE OF AMERICAN RABBIS

5780 NEW YORK 2020

Names: Yanklowitz, Shmuly, 1981- author.
Title: The book of Jonah : a social justice commentary / Rabbi Dr. Shmuly
    Yanklowitz ; consulting editors, Abraham J. Frost, Suzanne Bring, Judry
    Subar ; with a foreword by Christine Hayes, PhD.
Description: New York : Central Conference of American Rabbis, 2020. |
    Summary: "A social justice commentary of the Book of Jonah providing
    insights on ethical issues such as animal welfare, incarceration,
    climate change, and others"-- Provided by publisher.
Identifiers: LCCN 2020004247 (print) | LCCN 2020004248 (ebook) | ISBN
    9780881233605 (trade paperback) | ISBN 9780881233612 (ebook)
Subjects: LCSH: Bible. Jonah--Criticism, interpretation, etc. | Social
    justice--Biblical teaching.
Classification: LCC BS1605.52 .Y36 2020 (print) | LCC BS1605.52 (ebook) |
    DDC 224/.9206--dc23
LC record available at https://lccn.loc.gov/2020004247
LC ebook record available at https://lccn.loc.gov/2020004248

Book interior design and composition
by Scott-Martin Kosofsky at The Philidor Company,
Rhinebeck, NY

10 9 8 7 6 5 4 3 2 1 0

CCAR Press, 355 Lexington Avenue, New York, NY 10017
(212) 972-3636 . ccarpress@ccarnet.org
www.ccarpress.org

Publication of this book
is made possible in part
by the generosity of
The Esther S. and Hyman J. Bylan
Memorial Fund.

This book is dedicated to my amazing children,

Amiella Rachel

Meir Lev Kook

Maya Neshama

Shaya Or Nafshi Yosef

I love you with all my heart. Along with your wonderful mother, Shoshana, you are my dearest and most precious gifts. Each day, you radically illuminate our lives with love and meaning. We are so blessed to be your parents. You sweeten our lives. May you each be blessed to always have calm, quiet, and prayerful spaces of refuge inside "fishes" of your own. May you live your divine mission out in the world, actualize your deepest values, provide support for the other and the stranger, and know that wherever the sea may take you, you should let your heart follow, too.

Contents

Foreword

IN 2015, I WAS INVITED by Shmuly Yanklowitz to speak at Valley Beit Midrash, a collaborative organization offering Jewish educational and leadership programming in the Greater Phoenix area. When I arrived in Arizona in April 2016, I was greeted by an irrepressible visionary.

Anyone who has had the good fortune to interact with Rav Shmuly can attest to his boundless energy, his grounded spirituality, and his inspiring Torah. A passionate social justice activist and an indefatigable teacher, Rav Shmuly, through his words and actions, exudes a deep kindness and profound love for his fellow creatures. These are the very qualities that radiate from the pages of Rav Shmuly's extended meditation on the biblical Book of Jonah.

The questions raised by the Book of Jonah are searingly relevant today, and it is for this reason that Shmuly Yanklowitz has chosen the Book of Jonah as the jumping-off point for an unflinching exploration of the most urgent moral issues of our time, offering himself as guide and partner. Like the Book of Jonah itself, Rav Shmuly's meditations are deeply Jewish and deeply human. His book speaks to any person gripped by the overwhelming challenges of the twenty-first century; he draws wisdom not only from traditional Jewish sources, but also from biblical scholarship and from writings dedicated to social justice philosophy, moral psychology, and more. In these pages, readers will probe the problem of theodicy, the complex nature of truth, the danger of fundamentalist absolutism, the power and pitfalls of compassion, and the dynamic character of the biblical God. In Rav Shmuly's hands, the Book of Jonah provides insights that illuminate such contemporary ethical issues as animal welfare, incarceration, climate change, weapons of mass destruction, and Jewish-Muslim relations.

But there is more, for one detects in every line of Rav Shmuly's writing a sense of urgency. It is the same urgency found in God's opening call to Jonah, a call to join in repairing a broken world, a call that we—unlike Jonah—must hasten to answer.

Jonah is a perplexing figure who flees from God's plan for a better world—not because he fears God's justice, but because he resents God's mercy. Despite moments of introspection—one within the dark recesses of a great fish and one by the side of a withered plant—Jonah remains an enigma. Does he ever reconcile himself to God's love for all Creation, or does he continue to value truth and strict justice over compassion and mercy? This is, in essence, the question God poses in the final verse of this little book, and though the question is directed at Jonah, it is also addressed to the book's readers. Having witnessed the unfolding drama, where do *we* stand on the questions that divide God and Jonah? How do *we* manage the tension between justice and mercy? How do *we* feel about second chances? How do *we* balance particularism and universalism? How do *we* negotiate competing truth claims in a world of human diversity? And how will *we* respond to the call to repair a broken world? When the Book of Jonah closes, God is waiting for the prophet's answer.

Rav Shmuly reminds us—urgently—that God is waiting, still, for our answer.

—*Christine Hayes, PhD*
    Robert F. and Patricia Ross Weis Professor
    of Religious Studies in Classical Judaica,
    Yale University

Acknowledgments

THE PROCESS OF RETRACING Jonah's steps afforded me the unique opportunity to glimpse into the mind of a prophet and reconsider my preconceived notions on a vast array of issues. Jonah's world, while seemingly far from our own, offered insights into the condition of contemporary society and the need to recommit to spiritual excellence and moral rigor.

Jonah's status and role as a prophet has always intrigued me, and I am thankful that after so many years, I have been given the blessed opportunity to explore the lessons of his life at length. Publishing a book is no easy feat. It takes a lot of time, patience, love, care, and the strength to keep pushing. Throughout the process of researching and writing this book, I was blessed to have had many people at my side who granted me the encouragement and strength. First, I am grateful to my publisher, CCAR Press, for allowing me to contribute another book to their library of Jewish literature. When I published my commentary on *Pirkei Avot* through CCAR, I was blown away by their professionalism, their attentiveness, and their commitment to ensure that my work was seen by the widest possible audience. It was, simply put, an amazing experience. To Rabbi Hara Person, thank you for being my guiding light at the CCAR, and to Rabbi Sonja K. Pilz, PhD, thank you for your superb editing work. Many thanks as well to Raquel Fairweather, Deborah Smilow, Leta Cunningham, and the rest of the CCAR Press team for their support. Debra Corman copy edited the manuscript, Michelle Kwitkin proofread it, Scott-Martin Kosofsky designed the text, and Barbara Leff designed the cover. I'd like to extend my gratitude as well to CCAR Press's interns: Janet Katz, Rachel Pass, Arielle Salomon, and Leah Ritterband. I am truly grateful for everything CCAR does.

I'm also grateful for the attentive work of Abraham J. Frost, who spent numerous hours editing drafts, offering constructive feedback, and providing support. I am grateful to Suzanne Bring, who added enormous insight with her contributions and editing acumen; and to Judry Subar, who contributed important edits as well, for his diligence. The assistance of these esteemed colleagues was invaluable as I embarked on my journeys with Jonah.

Most importantly, this book would not have been possible without the everlasting love of my beautiful and brilliant wife, Shoshana, and our wonderful children, Amiella, Lev, Maya, and Shay. Whenever I found myself in need of inspiration, I thought of my family. Thank you for all the joy and light you share with me on a daily basis. I love you endlessly!

Finally, I give my humble thanks to the Creator—the One True God—for giving me life, for giving me hope, for giving me challenges to overcome, and for giving me the ability to pursue a life dedicated to holiness.

Introduction:
What Happens in the Book of Jonah?

THE BOOK OF JONAH is located within the Twelve Minor Prophets of the *Tanach*. Among the shortest books in the Bible at forty-eight verses, it also seems to take place over the course of just a week or two: there are three days in a fish, three days on a journey to Nineveh, and not much between them. The story takes place in a large Mesopotamian city during the reign of Jeroboam II[1] (roughly in the eighth or seventh century BCE).[2]

The Book of Jonah is filled with seeming contradictions, an unreliable central character, and a nature-defying centerpiece; it recounts tales of punishment and forgiveness, but it is not a book of law. Jonah, the central prophet, lacks a certain quality of candor. The narrative is so vibrant and sincere that its theological ramifications seem almost an afterthought.

Like the Homeric works of *The Iliad* and *The Odyssey*, the Book of Jonah explores what happens when people fail to live up to their heroic potential. God instructs Jonah, a Jewish prophet, to call upon the gentile population of Nineveh to repent. Rather than charge forward, Jonah flees from his mission, escaping on a ship. While Jonah is aboard, God brings on a mighty storm, shaking the ship's passengers both physically and spiritually. The sailors, fearing that the divine wrath will take them to their deaths, toss Jonah overboard after he admits that he is the impetus of the storm. God performs a miracle, however, and saves Jonah inside the belly of a great fish. For three days and three nights, Jonah prays until he is released. After his release from the fish, Jonah fulfills his mission, albeit reluctantly. Jonah calls upon the citizens of Nineveh to repent, and they oblige. God spares the city from destruction.

Jonah's story ends with him in isolation, far from Nineveh. He cries out to God, expressing frustration and castigating God for sending him on an unwanted mission. In order to teach Jonah the meaning of loving-kindness, God grows a plant that provides Jonah with shade from the blazing sun—and then God lets it wither away, leaving Jonah vulnerable to the elements. God explains to Jonah that God cares about the people of Nineveh just as Jonah had cared about the plant—and confronts him with the fact that the universal nature of divine love and concern for a large city might well exceed Jonah's depression over the death of a plant. The word *gadol* ("large, great") is the most frequent word in the short book, appearing fourteen times. Abraham Ibn Ezra (c. 1089–1167, Spain) suggests that Nineveh is described as "a great city to God" because its citizens had been righteous in the past, before straying toward wickedness.[3] Had they always been wicked, Ibn Ezra argues, God would not have bothered to send a prophet to urge repentance. Only because they had so recently strayed were they deemed worthy of a second chance.

The Book of Jonah and Its Classical Commentaries

A rabbinic teaching[4] shares that Jonah was the child that the prophet Elijah brought back to life (I Kings 17:19–22). Whether Jonah actually lived or this tale should be read as symbolic, he is a mesmerizing figure. While the Book of Kings (II Kings 14:25) calls Jonah "Yonah ben Amitai *hanavi*,"[5] the Book of Jonah surprisingly never actually designates Jonah a prophet. Yet, as Professor Mark Kleinman writes:

> Jonah is a strange prophet: without insight, without foresight, without compassion, and without courage. Most of all, he is without energy and without initiative: throughout, he seems oddly passive. A modern diagnosis might be depression, or at least dysthymia.[6]

While other prophets are initially reluctant to fulfill their prophetic duty, Jonah is the only prophet in the Hebrew Bible who actively attempts to escape his divinely-mandated prophetic mission.[7] He flees to the Diaspora. He flees to the bottom of the ship. He constantly runs from God. But the Book of Jonah does not only tell the story of a rebellious prophet; it may be the story of the most successful one as well. In the end, it takes merely five words to turn Nineveh's entire populace toward complete repentance.[8] However, it may be unfair to compare prophets to one another.

There are many interpretations of Jonah's flight from responsibility. Rabbi Isaac Abarbanel (1437–1508, Portugal) argues that Jonah was not only justified but heroic in his defiance of God, because he did so to save the Jewish people of the Northern Kingdom of Israel. Jonah was worried that the Ninevites, rather than repent, would kill the Jews, as Nineveh was the capital of Assyria, an enemy of the Kingdoms of Judah and Israel (respectively the Southern and Northern Kingdoms).[9] Abarbanel also writes that Jonah fled not from God but from prophecy.[10]

A quite different question arises when we ponder Jonah's behavior from a psychological viewpoint. Does he have what we now call bipolar disorder? Abarbanel interprets "He lay down and fell asleep" (1:5) to mean that Jonah thought he would die on the ship, referring to the Talmudic statement that sleep is one-sixtieth of death.[11] To me, it seems possible that Jonah is actually depressed; going to sleep at times of enormous stress can be a dysfunctional coping mechanism. One sleeps to escape reality. When the captain says to Jonah, "What is this to you, O sleeping one?" he is asking a rhetorical question. More than anything else, he expresses his surprise over Jonah's unusual reaction. How can someone possibly sleep at such a perilous time? After all, the lives of all aboard the ship are in danger!

A well-known *midrash* explains:

> If one Jew sins, all of Israel feels it. . . . This can be compared to the case of men on a ship, one of whom took a drill and began drilling beneath his own place. His fellow travelers said to him, "What are you doing?" He replied, "What does that matter to you? I am drilling only under my own place." They continued, "We care because the water will come up and flood the ship for us all."[12]

This notion of individual actions having reverberating effects perhaps can be extended to any society, and not just the Jewish community. The Book of Jonah is unusual for Hebrew Bible in part because it's about Nineveh, a city where Jews do not reside.[13]

The Book of Jonah: God's Universal Ethics

Not long ago, I was on an airplane for a business trip to scenic New Jersey. It began as a rather routine flight, nothing particularly striking, until I took out my book on the history of Nineveh (where the Book of Jonah is set) and the gentleman sitting next to me said, "That's my hometown!" My traveling companion, it turns out, was a Christian Iraqi refugee from Mosul.[14] We got to chatting. What ensued made for, perhaps, the most fascinating flight I have ever taken. I do not usually drink hard liquor, but after the fellow asked several times if I would share a drink with him, I finally agreed to have a little rum. It happened that across the aisle, another Christian fellow wanted to talk about Jonah and about the geography and history of Nineveh. Shortly, the front of the plane was having a blast learning Torah and making *l'chayims*—toasts to life. Had he been there with us, Jonah ben Amitai himself would have gotten a real kick out of the scene unfolding!

God's concern for the non-Jewish metropolis reminds us that Judaism understands God as the God of all humanity, rather than only as the God of the Jews (Psalm 145:9). God is concerned with the 120,000 people living in Nineveh regardless of their religion. Even more surprising: custom prescribes that this book be recited on Yom Kippur, the day that stands at the pinnacle of the Jewish calendar.[15]

The reasoning of the compilers of the Yom Kippur liturgy is enthralling: From this book, we learn about *t'shuvah*—literally, "return [to an original state]." The term is often translated as human "transformation," "repentance," or "growth"—God's concern for all creatures, and the delicate balance of creating a world both with *middat hadin* ("judgment") and *middat rachamim* ("compassion"). The Book of Jonah offers particularistic wisdom, though it is almost entirely concerned with universalistic lessons such as repentance and mercy.

We are assured on Yom Kippur that just as God prefers *rachamim* ("mercy") over *din* ("judgment") for Jonah and Nineveh, so will God continue to show us mercy. The High Holy Day prayers say that God is "merciful and gracious, slow to anger, and abundant in kindness and truth" (*rachum v'chanun erech apayim v'rav chesed ve'emet*; Exodus 34:6). But the Book of Jonah omits "and truth" (*ve'emet*), suggesting that God may be soft-hearted and kind but insufficiently committed to truth and judgment. We learn that none of us would be able to withstand God's truth and judgment: "If God were to judge [strictly by the book], no one could withstand" (Psalm 130:3). Rather, we should learn not to judge others, because we do not wish to be judged. We should emulate God, who judges mercifully rather than harshly.

God gives Jonah another chance, even after Jonah's repeated defiance. God does not remind Jonah of his sin of fleeing from responsibility; rather, God assumes that Jonah repents. This remains a Jewish tradition: one should not remind others of their past wrongs (based on Leviticus 19:17). Considering the nature of the repentance in Nineveh,[16] the sages teach that if one steals a beam and builds upon it a great building, we should not undermine the entire building to return the beam to its owner.[17]

The book possibly tells us more about God than about Jonah. God continues to talk to Jonah despite Jonah's obstinacy and disobedience. God does not cast Jonah away, instead demonstrating patience and mercy. Psychologically and theologically, it may be difficult to grasp, but the Book of Jonah teaches that nature is in God's control: the sea, the great fish, the wind, the *kikayon* plant, all of it.

A master of apologetics might assert that God is perfect and immutable, but this is not the God of the Torah. The God of the Hebrew Scriptures is a God who changes and repents. As humans evolve, God evolves with them. This dynamic relationship gives the human enterprise great significance: "God created worlds and destroyed them, created worlds and destroyed them, until God arrived at this world."[18] Everything is a vehicle for God's revelation and interaction with the world. Even the thorniness of Jonah's life is useful in helping us understand the mysterious forces that influence the universe.

The Book of Jonah: A Biblical Message of Human Responsibility in a Shared World

The Book of Jonah may be a product of imagination of Jewish power in the world. Jonah utters just a few words, but the whole world listens. Yet, the Book of Jonah also demonstrates the timeless tension Jews have with neighboring nations. Are we one of them? Are we friendly but separate? Are we enemies? Even more, what is the relationship between our moral and spiritual convictions, and theirs? As biblical scholar Avivah Zornberg (b. 1944) notes, "The book of Jonah invites interpretation from the first verse to the last; but its elusive meanings are never fully netted. There is no conclusive answer to its questions."[19] Thus, Jonah—both the book and the character—has been subject to countless interpretations.

Many early Christian commentators,[20] who held deeply antisemitic views,[21] saw the Book of Jonah as a model for why Christianity was superior to the earlier—and in their view, more barbaric—Judaism.[22] Christianity, they argued, was built on a universalist foundation, concerned with the souls of all humans, while Judaism, as they thought Jonah demonstrated, is only concerned with Jews.[23] They suggest that Jonah rejects God's call to Nineveh to repent because the people of Nineveh were not Jewish. For them, Jonah was the quintessential ethnocentric tribalist that Christianity comes to uproot and replace—a critique of the affluent and self-centered Jews living in Jerusalem during the time of the early kings of Israel (when the book is traditionally believed to have been written) who viewed themselves as the recipients of God's favor. They, like Jonah, might have wondered, "Why should the gentiles be saved?" When God sends a prophet, even a reluctant one such as Jonah, to save the Assyrian Empire, it serves to countermand the tribalism inherent to the Israelite kings.[24] In response, Jewish commentators argued that Jonah had better, or at least other, reasons to deny God's call.

One might ask why a book about a prophet who flees God's call should be included among the Hebrew Scriptures at all. Rabbi David Kimchi, known as Radak (1160–1235, France), writes:

> [The Book of Jonah] was written to be a moral lesson to Israel, for a foreign nation that is not part of Israel was ready to repent, and the first time a prophet rebuked them, they turned to a complete repentance from evil.[25]

Erica Brown further explains Radak's interpretation:

> His comments sting with their truth. Radak, following in his critique, suggests that Jonah fled so as not to bring punishment on his people, thereby demonstrating more honor for the Israelites than he showed toward God. . . . He also mentions the *Aggadah* that Jonah received prophecy twice but not three times because of his obvious failings as a prophet (see Babylonian Talmud, *Yevamot* 98a). Yet he softens the blow by adding another lesson based on Jonah's miraculous salvation in a fish belly twinned with God's compassion for Nineveh: "God, who is blessed, is merciful to those who repent from any nation and grants them mercy, even more so when they are many" (Radak to Jonah 1:1).[26]

Women share in human responsibility, but there are no women mentioned in the entirety of the Book of Jonah. Sailors, a king, a prophet, 120,000 city people of Nineveh—but no women. Who was Jonah's wife? His mother? Does he have any family or friends at all? While the book doesn't mention Jonah's wife, the Talmud does. The rabbis say that Jonah's wife would ascend to Jerusalem for the three festivals each year (Passover, Shavuot, and Sukkot).[27] The biblical book also does not mention his mother, but the rabbis do. They suggest that his mother was the widow Zarephat who entertained Elijah[28] and whose son Elijah resuscitated (Jonah).[29] Perhaps it is just for this reason that Jonah leads from such a narrow place. He appears to have no family, no friends, no soul mate. If a fifth chapter to the Book of Jonah were to be written, it might be a feminist chapter that reimagines a future where women are not only present, but in positions of leadership.

Though it is brief, Jonah's story is not particularly easy to digest. The book's moral ambiguity requires guidance.[30] For example, Erica Brown notes the significance of Jonah moving eastward:

> Eastward is never a positive direction, biblically speaking; this is true from the very first chapters of Genesis. Eastward suggests a movement away from goodness and intimacy, from holiness and purposeful existence. It affirms that this is a book to be taken seriously as a theological struggle between human beings and their Maker. [31]

One reason to be empathetic toward Jonah is that leadership is difficult. President John F. Kennedy wrote about this shocking dynamic when becoming president: "When we got into office, the thing that surprised me the most was that things were as bad as we'd been saying they were."[32] We cannot be sufficiently prepared for the challenges of leadership.

Rabbi Lord Jonathan Sacks writes:

> Even the greatest were reluctant to lead. Moses at the burning bush found reason after reason to show that he was not the man for the job. Isaiah and Jeremiah both felt inadequate. Summoned to lead, Jonah ran away. The challenge really is daunting. But when you feel as if you are being called to a task, if you know that the mission is necessary and important, then there is nothing you can do but say *Hineni*, "Here I am."[33]

Does God condemn Jonah for his initial refusal? Certainly not. In Hebrew, Jonah's name means "dove." James Ackerman, professor emeritus at Indiana University, suggests:

> The dove has two major characteristics in the Hebrew Bible: it is easily put to flight and seeks secure refuge in the mountains (Ezekiel 7:16, Psalm 55:6–8), and it moans and laments when in distress (Nahum 2:7, Isaiah 38:14, 59:11). Will these characteristics, we wonder, also apply to our hero?[34]

Doves are harbingers of peace and symbols of God's capacity to forgive—a characteristic that dominates the Book of Jonah. After Jonah rejects God's call, he is not struck down or discharged. Instead, God affords him, who seemingly lacks faith, a second chance.

Probably each one of us can relate to the need for second chances, both in our daily lives and in our moral and spiritual lives before God. Ultimately, Jonah's book is written for us, regular people who live in the world each day and wonder if we can make it through unharmed. We battle everyday leviathans simply to make our lives worthwhile and the world safe for our children and loved ones. Even with our limited understanding and finite lives, we are called to look not only after our own needs, but also at the broader picture. Jonah is no different from you or me. We learn from him to give and take second chances with compassion, as well as that, in spite of our own personal desires, it is not acceptable to escape our human responsibilities in this shared world.

Author's Note

IN THE MIDST of the uncertainty of today's world, a book asking us to reflect on our internal spiritual qualities is more important and timely than ever. I want this book to be both scholarly and accessible, as I do not think that sufficient attention has been paid to Jonah and his story within today's academic and theological discourses. Many of us are still intimidated by the inherent strangeness of this prophet and his ordeal.

My goal is for this book to apply traditional Jewish knowledge to our contemporary world and questions. I want to bring forth an inspiring book that conveys Jonah's deeds to a twenty-first century audience, regardless of background, ancestry, or affiliation. To this aim, I stray a bit from line-by-line commentary, as well as from a straight historical reading. Translations in the chapters are my own. The full text of the Book of Jonah appears at the end of this volume. The Hebrew text and English translation are from the Jewish Publication Society.

Jonah's actions can become beacons for social justice and universal responsibility in Jewish social justice philosophy. Jonah's world comes alive by tying his trials and tribulations—and his responses to these tests—to moral and spiritual issues of our current moment. Over the course of this book, his struggle between Jewish universalism and particularism, with the moral responsibility we have toward the stranger, his lack of understanding evil and his protesting God, his prayer, his spirituality, and his moral development become metaphors for our time.

My hope is that readers of this book begin reading with questions and end with even more questions, yearning to think and learn more. I also hope that this book will deepen the experience of Yom Kippur, as well as our ongoing practice of inner reflection: How we can become better neighbors, community members, spiritual beings, or, simply, people? Every sunrise brings us a fresh opportunity for introspection and healing. Can each of us find a little bit of Jonah within us? Are we prepared to heed our calls?

Let us begin the adventure.

CHAPTER 1

Religious Activism
God's Commandments and Our Responsibility

Go at once to Nineveh, that great city, and proclaim judgment
upon it, for their wickedness[35] has come before Me.
—Jonah 1:2

WHAT DOES IT MEAN TO PROTEST?

Protesting expresses the opinion that there is something wrong with the ways of the world. At the same time, an act of protest is also an optimistic step to take, signifying our conviction that human actions can be held accountable, human institutions fixed, and society changed. Protest attempts to fight inequity, hatred, greed, and maybe even fear.

Why is this relevant?

The Book of Jonah opens with the idea that religious actions can be politically subversive. In the first two verses, God calls upon Jonah to become a religiously motivated political activist: God speaks to Jonah and implores him to remonstrate against an unjust society. While we often imagine public political protest to be a secular phenomenon, in the Book of Jonah God calls upon the prophet to initiate religious action.

Contemporary activists often use strategies of community organizing to create an active and broad grassroots movement. However, our Hebrew prophet, Jonah, acted alone. In our story, there is only Jonah—and his opponent, Nineveh, "that great city."[36] One can only imagine how overwhelmed he must have felt by God's command. Without offering the reader any background on Jonah's morality or prophetic capacity, the book opens by describing his daunting task. How can a single man from a small people be asked to stand up to the great Assyrian Empire—specifically, to the 120,000 people of Nineveh? Who would *not* run from such a massive request? Today, as during Jonah's time, religious activists rarely find themselves prepared for the monumental challenges lying before them.

To protest means to publicly declare that injustice and bigotry are unacceptable and that callousness must never be tolerated. Bearing witness and protesting are not just moral acts, but also deeply religious ones.[37] In the Jewish tradition, we are obligated at times to offer *tochechah* ("reproof, rebuke") when others are acting unethically. The Book of Leviticus says, "You shall not hate your kinsfolk in your heart. Reprove your kin but incur no guilt on their account" (Leviticus 19:17). This verse suggests three necessary elements to your rebuke to make it effective and not hurtful:

1. Rebuke only in situations that oblige you to rebuke.[38]
2. Rebuke in order to not hate the other.
3. Use your rebuke to prevent any negative feelings from festering.

Political activism requires that we evaluate our tactics to ensure that we choose the most impactful ones. Political activism is thus generally utilitarian—oriented toward results. Protest, in contrast to other forms of political activism, is deontological; we protest because we are religiously obliged to. Even if protest produces neither an immediate result nor any measurable impact, we still have a moral and religious mandate to protest against injustice.

Yet it cannot be denied that protest is a delicate subject. Historically, there have been times when Jewish minority populations faced prejudice and physical threats and dangers. The desire to advocate for an end to injustice was checked by the practical need to survive under harsh conditions. Yet, standing idly by while others suffer has always been an insufficient response to world events. As if to address the tension between the obligation to public protest and the threats and dangers that it poses, Maimonides (b. ca. 1135, Cordoba; d. 1204, Cairo) reminds us that sometimes protest is most effective when done privately:

If you see that someone committed a sin or walks in a way that is not good, it is your responsibility to bring the mistaken one back to the right path and point out that such a person is doing wrong to themself by this evil course. . . . One who condemns another, whether for offenses against people or for sins against God, should scold in private, speak to the offender gently and tenderly, and point out that the criticism is offered for the person's own good, to secure life in the World-to-Come. If the person accepts the rebuke, well and good. If not, the person should be rebuked a second and a third time. And so one is obligated to continue the critiques until the sinner confronts the rebuker and says, "I refuse to listen." Whoever is in a position to prevent wrongdoing and does not do so is responsible for the sins of all the wrongdoers whom that person might have stopped.[39]

So, we see that protest can take several forms in Judaism. It can be either a public act or a private rebuke. In addition, protest—"standing up to injustice"—can be a form of prayer. Indeed, this is how Jewish tradition describes its beginnings:

[The patriarch] Abraham instituted the morning prayer;[40] as it is said, "Abraham rose early in the morning and [went] to the place where he had previously stood" (Genesis 19:27)—there is no "standing" that is not prayer.[41]

When one "stands" or when one "takes a stand," that is prayer. Abraham's "stand" against the destruction of Sodom and Gomorrah is a source of inspiration for future Jewish activists, for Jews taking a stance against injustice.

In addition to protest as a private act, public rebuke, or prayer, protest is also a form of promoting self-growth. We remind ourselves of our priorities. We remind ourselves of our "capacity for outrage," a power often lost to the malaise of indifference. Rabbi Abraham Joshua Heschel (1907–1972) once lamented over the increasing indifference in these words:

O Lord, we confess our sins, we are ashamed of the inadequacy of our anguish, of how faint and slight is our mercy. We are a generation that has lost its capacity for outrage. We must continue to remind ourselves that in a free society all are involved in what some are doing. Some are guilty, all are responsible.[42]

We protest simply because we dare not be silent. The rabbis teach that "silence is acquiescence," and rabbinic sources repeatedly indicate that political activism toward a more just and equitable society is incumbent upon us all:

Everyone who can protest [the sin of] one's household and does not, is punished [i.e., responsible] for the [the sin of the] people of one's household. [Anyone who can protest the sin of] the people of one's town [and does not], is punished for the [sin of the] people of one's town. [Anyone who can protest the sin of] the whole world [and does not], is punished for the [sin of the] whole world.[43]

Anyone can protest,[44] but it takes influential voices for the protest to be heard and cause political change. Indeed, the rabbis believed that there was an increased obligation for scholars and leaders to engage, organize, and sacrifice themselves in the spirit of righteous protest:

As long as one is but an ordinary scholar, he has no concern with the congregation and is not punished [for its lapses], but as soon as he is appointed head and dons the cloak [of leadership], he must no longer say: "I live for my own benefit, I care not about the congregation," but the whole burden of the community is on his shoulders. If he sees a person causing suffering to another, or transgressing, and does not prevent him, then he is held punishable.[45]

But we do not always have to follow leaders. Each of us can choose to take a stand. Consider how some American rabbis in the mid-twentieth century described their compulsion to act during the height of the civil rights movement:

We came because we could not stand idly by our brother's blood. We had done that too many times before. We have been vocal in our exhortation of others but the idleness of our hands too often revealed an inner silence. . . . We came as Jews who remember the millions of faceless people who stood quietly, watching the smoke rise from Hitler's crematoria. We came because we know that second only to silence, the greatest danger to man is loss of faith in man's capacity to act.[46]

Is religious activism an integral part of contemporary Jewish identity? At many times in Jewish history, Jews have had to live as second-class citizens in non-Jewish cultures, dependent on the good grace of the non-Jewish ruling power. Today, Jews in the United States live with the perspective of being both insiders and outsiders to contemporary American society. We are conscious of being insiders, accepted in almost every way.[47] Yet, we often perceive of ourselves as outsiders, a perception based on millennia of exclusion and discrimination. This gives us a unique role in contemporary American society. We have access to power and privilege, yet we also remember our obligation to advocate for those at the margins of society. Intervention on behalf of the vulnerable is both necessary to change the current societal reality and essentially Jewish:

> From where do we know that if we see another person drowning, mauled by beasts, or attacked by robbers, that we are bound to save them? The Torah teaches, "You shall not stand idly by the blood of your neighbor" (Leviticus 19:16).[48]

Judaism demands involvement and responsibility. We must bear witness to injustice, and then we must act to stave off the ill effect of injustice on humanity. Action in the face of cruelty is a moral and religious act.[49] God commands us to submit ourselves to religious morality and ethics and to rebel against what we know to be wrong in this world. Jewish dietary laws, in whatever form we might embrace them, can be seen as a protest against greed, mindless consumption in the face of hunger, and cruelty toward animals. The laws of the Sabbath can be interpreted as protest against worker abuse, animal torture, and environmental degradation. Fast days can serve as protests against the grind of daily existence without reflection. Judaism reminds us that in all we do, we must be intentional, be sensitive to injustice, and aim for change.

Anyone can and should step up to address any given situation.

However, *we*—each of us individually and all of us as the Jewish community—need to have the courage to stand up when it is on us.

The idea of standing and speaking up, even when the consequences may be dire, is the foundation for Purim.[50] During Purim, we are reminded of the bravery it takes to it stand up for what is right and the peril of remaining hushed when our lives are on the line:

> On the contrary, if you keep silent in this crisis, relief and deliverance will come to the Jews from another quarter, while you and your father's house will perish. And who knows, perhaps you have attained to royal position for just such a crisis. (Esther 4:14)

This leads us back to Jonah, who, though an enigmatic human being, had a clear spiritual mission. Jonah is tasked with a difficult burden: to speak truth to the wicked in order to save their civilization and redeem their souls. It is a seemingly insurmountable challenge. His divinely mandated protest is not merely to fulfill a social duty, but rather to inspire change, change that will save tens of thousands of lives—of Israel's enemies.

The Hebrew Scriptures emphasize over and over again the absolute importance of God's laws and ethics and our limitless responsibility to live according to them. The late Torah scholar Nahum Sarna (1923–2005, England/United States) writes:

> It is not the neglect of sacrificial gifts, the disregard of an oracular utterance, or the making of a false oath that arouses the ire of the Deity. The sins are entirely on a moral plane, and of idolatry there is not so much as a whisper. As with the Flood (Genesis 6), the Sodom and Gomorrah narrative (Genesis 18–19) is predicated upon the existence of a moral law of universal application for the infraction of which God holds all men answerable. The idea that there is an intimate, in fact, inextricable connection between the socio-moral condition of a people and its ultimate fate is one of the main pillars upon which stands the entire Biblical interpretation of history. The theme is central to the Flood story, basic to the Sodom and Gomorrah narrative and fundamental to the understanding of the Book of Jonah.[51]

Many of us may feel that we do not do enough. We may feel exhausted and tired of carrying the heavy weight of that universal responsibility. That's not just us. We see that even a prophet can feel similarly, and in response, he tries to run away from his responsibility.[52]

Jonah is us. We are Jonah.

It is not easy to be a prophet. The prophet is neither cool nor popular; the prophet is not the life of the party. The prophet is an anxious personality juggling the demands of God with the needs of humans. Constantly risking alienation or even death, the prophet is isolated and lonely.

But we are not allowed to turn away.

CHAPTER 2
God Calls Upon Jonah
Shouldering Our Responsibility

> *Jonah, however, started out to flee to Tarshish from the service*
> *of the Eternal. He went down to Jaffo and found a ship going*
> *to Tarshish. He paid the fare and went aboard to sail with the*
> *others to Tarshish, away from the service of the Eternal.*
> —Jonah 1:3

DESPITE THE CALL from on high to model righteousness for a morally compromised society, Jonah shirks responsibility. He flees.

This total rejection of responsibility is virtually unparalleled in *Tanach*, although there are others who decline to fulfill holy mandates. Already in the first chapters of Genesis, Adam and Eve hide from God (Genesis 3:8); later, Cain murders Abel and responds to God's query with "Am I my brother's keeper?" (Genesis 4:9); and many other examples follow.[53]

Jonah first rises, indicating his initial desire to respond—like most prophets before him—to God's question *Ayekah* ("Where are you?") with *Hineini* ("Here I am"). Yet, he turns the other way. Jonah was asked to "get up" (Jonah 1:2), but instead he goes "down" to Jaffo and then down even deeper when he is cast overboard into the sea (Jonah 1:3, 1:15). Modern biblical commentator Robert Alter writes, "For a brief moment, he might seem to be heeding God's command to get up and go to Nineveh, but this momentary illusion is broken by the infinitive 'to flee.'"[54] This is a remarkable and perplexing moment in the biblical story. Ibn Ezra writes:

> One wonders how there arose in the heart of a wise man, who knew God and God's deeds, the thought to flee from before God. For Jonah was in God's hand and the world is filled with God's glory.

How could he rebel against the prophetic command, since it is [specifically] stated [earlier] that he is "the prophet"?[55]

Joseph Campbell writes that if a hero does not heed the call to leadership, the "flowering world becomes a wasteland of dry stones."[56] The confidence of the masses and the hope of those on the brink of despair are shattered when leaders turn away from their moral task.

The first question we have to ask, then, is: Why? Why would Jonah flee from God's word?

Perhaps Jonah feels that prophecy should only by spoken in and to Israel, and that if he leaves the holy land God will no longer be able to call on him. Perhaps he feels that the people of Nineveh should not profit from God's care. However, Jonah learns that God will find him everywhere and that universal moral mandates are not restricted to one land.[57]

Alternatively, Jonah may flee not because he wants to run away from the prophecy and from divine closeness, but out of self-preservation. Maybe he believes that the people of Nineveh will not listen, but rather torture and kill him—a reasonable fear, given the facts that the Ninevites are the enemies of the Jews, that Jonah would become the messenger of bad tidings (Jonah 3:4), and that the words of many other Jewish prophets were also not well received.[58]

Why would a prophet who believes in the word of God be afraid? Would he not expect divine protection as a messenger in the employ of an omniscient God? Does Jonah not care to preserve the lives of the people of Nineveh?[59] Why does he shy away from pronouncing God's truth? In stopping Jonah's escape and forcing him to accept his prophetic duty, God is teaching a lesson of compassion.

It seems rather ironic that Jonah *ben Amitai* (literally: "person of truth") runs from God. However, a first hint to the answer to our question of the "why" might already be embedded within Jonah's name. *Yonah* (the "dove") represents peace (like the dove of peace in the Noah story), which might suggest that Jonah's reason to run away from his mission to enter the city of Israel's enemies might be his fear of conflict and violence; and *ben Amitai* suggests that the pursuit of truth might still be his highest value. Truth and peace are virtues often in tension with one another in the rabbinic tradition.[60] What he is called to do is not necessarily what he wants to do.

Some names describe one's nature; others describe one's destiny.

Jonah 1:3 offers insight into the human condition: when called to accountability, it is our instinct to hide or flee. Yet when we run away from God, we run from our responsibility to others and, ultimately, from ourselves and our true mission as human beings. In Jewish thought, running from God and running from people are intertwined. Emmanuel Levinas (1906–1995) writes, "The relation to God is already ethics . . . the proximity to God, devotion itself, is devotion to the other man."[61] Rabbi Abraham Isaac HaKohen Kook (1865–1935), the first Ashkenazic chief rabbi of British Mandate Palestine, writes:

> A world of chaos stands before us, all the time that we have not yet reached the *tikkun elyon*—"the highest level of healing, repairing, transforming"—by uniting all life forces and all their diverse tendencies. As long as each one exalts oneself, claiming, I am sovereign, I and no other—there cannot be peace in our midst.[62]

It is only when we recognize our ultimate responsibility to others that we are able to become our true selves—and live up to God's truth.

When Moses has his vision of the Burning Bush, any lingering doubt of his destiny evaporates. An angel appears to Moses, and Moses "gazed" (Exodus 3:2). Picking up on the superfluity of the phrasing (the word for sight is used twice), the sage Nachmanides (b. 1194, Spain; d. 1270, Palestine) writes:

> From the beginning, the angel Michael appeared to him as well as the Manifest Divine, but Moses did not see the Presence because he had not prepared his heart for prophecy, and when he inclined his heart and turned to see, the appearance of the Divine was revealed to him.[63]

Nachmanides explains that at this consequential moment in spiritual history, the greatest prophet in the Torah was not spiritually prepared. If Moses himself was not spiritually awake enough to notice the Burning Bush right before his eyes, how much are we missing each day? How many times a day does God call upon us, but we are deaf to God's voice? How many times does something beautiful appear right in front of our eyes, but we are blind to the miracle?[64] Not only do our deafness to God's voice and our blindness to the wonders of this world prevent us from enjoying the wonders of Creation, but they also keep us from recognizing our ultimate responsibilities.

Postmodernism teaches us to approach the world from the perspective of a skeptic—especially when it comes to human-made truths. However, many of us are struggling to preserve a sense of safety and clarity in such a world of indistinctness and uncertainty. In response to this struggle, Michael Fishbane, a contemporary American scholar of Jewish thought engaged in the work of constructive theology, has developed his "sacred attunement" theology:

> What is our primordial condition, to be recovered through reflection? Perhaps this: already with the opening of eyes, the hearing of ears, and the tactility of the body—already from such inadvertent moments the world imposes itself on us. It is always already there for me, just as I become there for it. There is no gap to be crossed (between the cognizing ego and the world): there is miraculously an immediate, primordial thereness of reality. Already from the first, and with every act of sensation, the world is "there" as a field of phenomenality, as a world of claims imposing themselves with an ever-present and evident presence. These claims put one under a primary obligation: one can respond or not respond; heal or destroy; attend or neglect; consume or build up. We have that choice.[65]

When we feel lost in the chaos of human truths, we should focus on ethical questions, the questions of our individual and collective responsibilities for God's Creation. Whenever we have courage not to hide but to respond, our response is *hineini*.[66] Rabbi Jonathan Sacks, the former chief rabbi of the United Kingdom, writes about each individual's unique responsibility:

There is no life without a task; no person without a talent; no place without a fragment of God's light waiting to be discovered and redeemed; no situation without its possibility of sanctification; no moment without its call. It may take a lifetime to learn how to find these things, but once we learn, we realize in retrospect that all it ever took was the ability to listen. When God calls, He does not do so by way of universal imperatives. Instead, He whispers our name—and the greatest reply, the reply of Abraham, is simply *hineini*: "Here I am," ready to heed Your call, to mend a fragment of Your all-too-broken world.[67]

One may commit major errors but still be worthy of hearing God's voice.[68] Out of fear and confusion, Jonah makes major errors, but God continues to speak to him.

Benedict (or Baruch) Spinoza (1632–1677), the excommunicated Enlightenment philosopher, writes that "fear cannot be without hope nor hope without fear."[69] The tendency to flee when danger is near is inherent to all mortal creatures. However, we also have the ability and responsibility to learn, listen, grow, and confront our fears. When fleeing God, we flee from moral responsibility, the sole source of human dignity, and the core of the human mission in this world. At our core is the light of our soul, created in the image of God. When we conceal that light and dismiss our human dignity, we forget our human responsibility.

Some people flee from their mission because they feel inadequate to the task. Others run from the task because they prioritize comfort, routine, and conformity over what they know is right or good. But to be religious means to be outraged. Rosa Parks (1913–2005) writes that she "learned over the years that when one's mind is made up, this diminishes fear; knowing what must be done does away with fear."[70]

Probably one of the strongest pulls away from our mission today is materialism. Perhaps Tarshish, known as a wealthy city,[71] represents the idolatry of the dollar that we see all too pervasive today.[72] James Ackerman writes:

> Jonah, a servant fleeing his master's sovereignty, also sees Tarshish as a refuge beyond YHWH's domain. Strangely, Tarshish also

connotes luxury, desire, delight. . . . For Jonah, therefore, Tarshish may paradoxically represent a pleasant place of security that borders on nonexistence.[73]

It may also be that whenever we are fleeing from our mission, we are actually running from our mortality. Ernest Becker (1924–1974), the twentieth-century Jewish American anthropologist, writes in *The Denial of Death*:

> Pascal's chilling reflection: "Men are so necessarily mad that not to be mad would amount to another form of madness." *Necessarily* because the existential dualism makes an impossible situation into an excruciating dilemma. *Mad* because, as we shall see, everything that man does in his symbolic world is an attempt to deny and overcome his grotesque fate. He literally drives himself into blind obliviousness with social games, psychological tricks, personal occupations so far removed from the reality of his situation that they are forms of madness—agreed madness, shared madness, disguised and dignified madness, but madness all the same.[74]

Whatever we are running from, we have to stop running. We are all here in this together. We need to learn that we cannot save ourselves as others perish. Only when each of us seizes our individual responsibility do we have a chance for all of us to live in dignity, in the image of God.

The rabbis taught about the verse "[God] wiped out all that existed on the face of the earth . . . there remained only Noah" (Genesis 7:23) that "Noah did not survive completely, for even he was coughing up blood because of the cold."[75] No "us versus them." We are in this world together; our lives are intertwined and so are our responsibilities!

We are to care not only about our own future but also about the fates of others. In *The Denial of Death*, Ernest Becker also writes:

> As Erich Fromm has so well reminded us . . . Freud discovered that each of us repeats the tragedy of the mythical Greek Narcissus: we are hopelessly absorbed with ourselves first of all. If we care about anyone it is usually ourselves first of all. As Aristotle somewhere put it: luck is when the guy next to you gets hit with the arrow.[76]

It is not easy to overcome the narcissistic illusion that as long as I am okay, all is well. Spiritual life is about awakening our inner selves from the fog of self-absorption. To be spiritual is to be awakened by what appears to us. Judaism is here to call us to our responsibility and to help us actualize our unique potential. Where Jonah fails, we can still succeed. The first step is choosing to be awake, to care, to see, and to hear the holy opportunities before us. We cannot flee from our challenges. We cannot flee from the responsibility to take ownership over our lives. We must answer the call. When we respond to the call, we remove our shame. When we stop hiding, we find our true selves.[77]

Perhaps Jonah the Prophet is merely a projection of our own fears and inadequacies. We face a world so demanding and daunting that we wish to run as far as we can. We go to sleep. When we wake up, it is as though we are still sleeping: filled with regrets over the past and anxieties about the future; unable to listen, internalize, and truly respond to the present.

When given the choice to run to Nineveh, where the work is crucial but hard, or to flee to Tarshish, where life may be easier, which choice do we make? This is a question we must ask ourselves each day as we realign ourselves with our deepest values.

CHAPTER 3

When We Get Hurt
Compassion as a Response to Theodicy

> *But the Eternal cast a mighty wind upon the sea, and such a*
> *great tempest came upon the sea that the ship was in danger of*
> *breaking up.*
> —Jonah 1:4

IN THE BOOK OF JONAH, God sends a mighty storm in order to end Jonah's flight, endangering the lives of many others on the ship. This storm raises many questions: Is God the ultimate cause of natural disasters? Why does God not care about the fear and pain the storm causes to other, entirely innocent people?

A *midrash* shares that the sailors saw other ships sailing peacefully while their own ship was fighting a fierce storm.[78] They correctly concluded that the fatal storm occurred in response to the sins of someone on their ship. Indeed, they perceived the storm as a divine punishment.

The enigma of theodicy (the theological problem of bad things happening to good people and vice versa) has long stymied theologians, philosophers, and lay people alike. In the Bible, there are many instances of senseless cruelty and abandonment: Cain murders Abel (Genesis 4:8), Hagar and Ishmael are left to die in the desert (Genesis 21:14–16), Pharaoh enslaves generations of innocent Hebrews (Exodus 1:8–10), Job endures calamity (Job 1–2). We, too, shout to the heavens: Where was God during the Holocaust?

How are we to respond to God's apparent silence and inaction?

We have learned that much of the suffering in our world is caused by human evil, which makes us ask: Why do innocent people have to suffer or die on the whims of the wicked? However, how does one

explain natural disasters such as earthquakes or cyclones,[79] or natural events like individual illnesses, which are clearly not in human
hands? Are those events in God's hands, or are they entirely random?
Most importantly, how can we continue to believe in a benevolent
and omnipotent God while so much suffering in the world still fes-
ters unattended? How does the eternal Divine interact with the delicate reality of human existence? Should not a God who proclaims
Godself a protector of all therefore keep all from harm?

These are not easy questions. There are no easy answers. We cannot explain why bad things happen to good people, but we can fight
against it. We can structure society such that the most vulnerable are
not left behind. In the face of suffering, Jewish tradition does not ask
us to be silent. Instead, we are to raise our voices toward the heavens
in the interest of those less fortunate than ourselves. The American
Bible scholar Yochanan Muffs (1932–2009) writes:

> Biblical religion does not seem to require the man of faith to repress
> his doubts in silent resignation. Abraham, Jeremiah, and Job, all
> men who question God's ways, are hardly numbered among the
> wicked. There is even some evidence that God demands such criti-
> cism, at least from His prophets (cf. Ezekiel 22:3).[80]

Jonah seems spiritually numb to his responsibilities toward the
innocent sailors on his ship. Rather than supporting them in their
fight against the waves or, even better, returning to his mission and
thereby saving their lives, he goes to sleep. The unnamed sailors on
the boat fervently and loyally pray for salvation—first to their own
gods (Jonah 1:5), and then to the God of Israel (Jonah 1:14). But
Jonah, the prophet, does not pray. Rather, he descends to the bottom
of the ship to sleep.[81] Why did Jonah not pray from below the ship as
well? Why did he simply go to sleep?

Rabbi Steven Bob meditates on the maturing relationship between
the sailors and God:

> Earlier, in verse 5, each sailor prayed to his own god. Here the
> sailors do not pray to their own gods; rather they pray to the one
> God of Israel, acknowledging the power of that God. They use the

four-letter name of The Eternal in their prayer. They have come to understand that YHVH truly rules the universe.[82]

Sickness, natural disasters, and other tragedies are inexplicable. Still, sometimes they inspire both courage and kindness in our fight to alleviate the suffering of others. Sadly, Jonah the Prophet is not an ideal model for an empathetic response to the suffering of others.

However, maybe we can make an effort to see Jonah through empathic eyes. Sometimes sleep is a sign of depression. Many, indeed, are paralyzed by the horrors of the world to the point they cannot do much more than sleep. We must be sensitive to that. The rest of us, though, should remain awake, alert, and ready to serve.

As Jews, we ought to do whatever we can to ease the suffering of others. I believe that this is what God wants us to do—while we might need to learn to live without answers to our ultimate questions.

How could you ease the suffering of others?

CHAPTER 4

Each Cried Out to Their Own God
On Religious Truth in a Pluralistic World

> *In their fright, the sailors cried out, each to his own god; and they flung the ship's cargo overboard to make it lighter for them. Jonah, meanwhile, had gone down into the hold of the vessel where he lay down and fell asleep.*
> —Jonah 1:5–6

I REPEATEDLY RETURN to one of Maimonides' most beautiful teachings—his introduction to his work on *Pirkei Avot*, called "The Eight Chapters,"[83] in which he writes that one can "accept *truth* from wherever one may find it."[84] Maimonides' sentiment is noble and forward-thinking: there is not simply one source of knowledge, but many. Such a concept seems simple, but it holds a certain tension: How do we differentiate between legitimate and illegitimate sources of truth? What separates truth from lie?

Jewish wisdom, as it has been handed down over the millennia, is certainly one place to seek *a version of truth*. But in our postmodern era, when truth is decentralized, uncertain, and conflict-driven, which truths matter for an individual's moral and spiritual journey?

This may seem to be a contemporary problem, but the collision among *multiple versions of truths* reaches back to the Bible. In the Book of Jonah, each sailor cried "to his own god," that is, to his own particular divine truth.[85] While the idea of diverse and seemingly antagonistic religions harmoniously coexisting in society may even today sound idealistic or simply ignorant, religious pluralism has a history that dates from antiquity. The sailors in the Book of Jonah were not merely seafaring together, but praying together, while peacefully maintaining their diversity.

As Jews, we do not want to pray to foreign gods and commit the sin of idolatry. We are tasked with the feat of respecting believers in the truths of other faiths who pray in their own languages, have their own names for God, and use their own prayer books.

Valuing *religious pluralism* means accepting that one's religion is not an exclusive source of truth, and acknowledging that different truths exist both in other religions and also in denominations within one's own religion. General pluralism necessitates and embraces interfaith efforts, strives for mutual respect, and values harmonious coexistence. Sociologists Peter Berger (1929–2017) and Anton Zijderveld (b. 1937) describe pluralism as a "situation in which diverse human groups (ethnic, religious, or however differentiated) live together under conditions of civic peace and in social interaction with each other."[86]

Those who embrace pluralism are demonstrating a certain humility and awareness of the vastness of the world. By embracing pluralism, we acknowledge that mere individuals cannot see the grand design. We need others, even those who are different from us and with whom we disagree, to help us understand the world around us. Both the human mind and the language it conjures are limited, and that which is used is a function of what people have encountered before. The challenge today is to keep from sliding into blind absolutism, where one's own truth is the only truth, or into a radical relativism, where there is no truth and no value in the pursuit of truth.

We see the beginnings of a concept of a *multiplicity of truths* in the writings of the prophets, such as the words of the prophet Micah:

> And the many nations shall go and shall say: "Come, let us go up to the mountain of the Eternal, to the House of the God of Jacob; that God may instruct us in God's ways, and that we may walk in God's paths." . . . Thus God will judge among the many peoples, and arbitrate for the multitudes of nations, however distant. . . . Everyone shall sit under their grapevine or fig tree with no one to disturb them. For it was the God of Hosts who spoke. Though all the peoples walk each in the name of its gods, we will walk in the name of the Eternal our God forever and ever. (Micah 4:2–5)

Rabbi Dr. Yitz Greenberg (b. 1933), a strong proponent of *Jewish pluralism*, argues for a unique approach to pluralistic religious thought:

> Pluralism means more than accepting or even affirming the other. It entails recognizing the blessings in the other's existence, because it balances one's own position and brings all of us closer to the ultimate goal. Even when we are right in our own position, the other who contradicts our position may be our corrective or our check against going to excess. . . . Pluralism is not relativism.[87]

The opposite of religious pluralism is *religious exclusivism*, which is the belief that only one religion or belief system can be true. Some think that many of the world's greatest injustices, including war, genocide, sacrifice, forced conversion, and conquest, are rooted in religious exclusivity.

However, in true interfaith encounters, we often discover that seeming conceptual differences are linguistic differences only and that seeming similarities often hide fruitful opposites. Sometimes, we get stuck on the level of mere language, especially in the face of inconsistencies. Certain language affirmations seem to reveal an immediate and accessible truth, while others appear to lead us astray. Hindus may say they believe in many gods, but Hindu theology actually does describe an ultimate source.

Rabbi Dr. Nathan Lopes Cardozo (b. 1946), my esteemed teacher and colleague, writes that indifference is often mistaken for tolerance:

> It is all too easy to espouse tolerance when one does not really care about values and principles, or about the moral needs of society and one's fellow man. In contrast, the stronger our convictions, the more tolerance we can show when we make the supreme sacrifice of listening to others and respecting their beliefs that we deem as incorrect. But to put up with others because we could not care less about their principles is not tolerance . . . it is a rubber spine.[88]

An exclusivist is one who is confident that their truth is the only truth and just engages others in order to convert them. It is possible for exclusivists to be compassionate and act kindly toward others they believe are misinformed.

In contrast, *religious inclusivism* asserts that while one's religion is still absolutely true, one can still learn to respect other religious systems of truth and learn bits of wisdom from other religions. This approach posits that Jews have much to learn outside of our own peoplehood and texts. A passage in the Talmud teaches that one can best understand the Torah by observing and learning from non-Jews.[89] Later, Maimonides makes it clear that righteous gentiles have a share in the World-to-Come.[90] This implies that certain elements in Jewish tradition support finding truth outside of the Torah and that God values the actions of non-Jews, such as the people of Nineveh, indicating that Jonah (and Jews in general) should learn also from non-Jews. The value of learning from non-Jewish peoples is a profound philosophical principle. Non-Jews can access God and religious truth. Radically, Maimonides argues that Christians and Muslims help straighten the path to the messianic age and repair the world so everyone can serve God together.[91]

Rabbi Lord Jonathan Sacks (b. 1948), himself a self-proclaimed inclusivist who rejects the seeming arbitrariness of pluralism, warns that exclusivity leads one to danger: "Universalism must be balanced with a new respect for the local, the particular, the unique."[92]

Likewise, Rabbi Joseph B. Soloveitchik (1903–1993) insisted that Jews embrace both their covenantal identity and their human identity:

> Jews have been burdened with a twofold task: we have to cope with the problem of a double confrontation. We think of ourselves as human beings, sharing the destiny of Adam in his general encounter with nature, and as members of a covenantal community which has preserved its identity under most unfavorable conditions, confronted by another faith community. . . . In this difficult role, we are summoned by God . . . to undertake a double mission—the universal human and the exclusive covenantal confrontation.[93]

For a religious person, there are essential truths outside of their own tradition that may help them better understand the truth of their own tradition. Pluralism is radical. Pluralism is daunting. Pluralism has the potential to shake off deeply rooted views. When approached respectfully, it greatly enhances our individual wisdom. Rabbi Eugene Borowitz (1924–2016) says that from a Jewish perspective, pluralism keeps the mind focused on the "primary human task," which is "creating holiness through righteousness. The responsible deed, the one that simultaneously acknowledges God, others, time, place, nature, and self . . . mends the torn [and] fulfills the promise inherent in existence."[94]

Pluralism is an approach that enables us, as Jews, to honor our own truths while dignifying the beliefs of others. This allows us to excel with intellectual rigor, expanded human solidarity, and religious humility.

Though he does not recognize it, while the sailors pray, Jonah has the opportunity to see firsthand the power of pluralism. He is given the unique opportunity to take a voyage with the people of the world and to learn and pray with them, but he instead hides below deck and sleeps.

We should be eager to build bridges and deepen respect and partnerships to bring repair to the world. Our task and our test is to value others without giving up our own values. We must embrace the diversity of our world, contribute what we as individuals and as a people have to offer, and above all, seek and accept truth wherever we may find it.

CHAPTER 5

When Sadness Strikes
Anxiety, Depression, Suicide, and Saving Angels

THE SAILORS ASK Jonah, "What should we do to you?" (Jonah 1:11). This is a humble question from a group reluctant to harm Jonah,[95] though he appears to be the cause of their peril.[96] The sailors show kindness to a complete stranger. Even after the fatal lot falls upon Jonah, they refuse to toss him into the sea. Instead, they engage in yet another task of discernment through inquiring about his background and actions (Jonah 1:8, 1:10). A *midrash* imagines that they lower him into the sea just a little to test the result of their lottery. When they lower Jonah into the water, the storm starts to subside, but when they raise him up, the storm returns immediately. They then try in vain to row furiously to get to dry land. It is Jonah who suggests that the shipmates throw him overboard (Jonah 1:12), which they eventually and hesitantly do (Jonah 1:15). Jonah seems to have given up on life entirely. How could he urge his own death when facing the goodwill of the sailors?[97]

Jewish legal sources on suicide and euthanasia differentiate between active measures ("pulling the plug") and passive measures (withholding life-sustaining treatment). Whereas we are absolutely forbidden from actively pursuing our own deaths, more passive measures are generally allowed to us. Similarly, Jonah is not willing to actively kill himself, but instead seeks others to do the deed for him. This will not be the last time that Jonah seeks death. Following the *t'shuvah* of Nineveh, Jonah is perplexed by God's compassion for the city and questions the point of his mission (Jonah 4:1–2). He cries out to God, "Please, Eternal, take my life, for I would rather die than live," and God responds, "Are you that deeply grieved?" (Jonah 4:3–4). Later on in that chapter, when the shade-giving plant provided by God withers, Jonah becomes faint from the heat and "begged for death, saying, 'I would rather die than live'" (Jonah 4:8). In the last chapter of the Book of Jonah, even God is perplexed by Jonah's returning wish to die: "Then God said to Jonah, 'Are you so deeply grieved about the plant?' 'Yes,' he replied, 'so deeply that I want to die'" (Jonah 4:9).

The narrative of Jonah's wish to extinguish his own life might be indicative of his mental health and point to a contemporary health crisis. Statistics about suicide in America today show a nation reeling from an epidemic of depression, isolation, and loneliness. According to a survey of suicide from the National Institutes of Mental Health, nearly forty-five thousand Americans died from suicide in 2016, and nearly one million people attempted suicide that year.[98] Suicide has increased dramatically over the last several decades, with nearly every state showing increases in self-inflicted death, according to the Centers for Disease Control.[99]

What should be the Jewish response to this crisis? How can we better understand suicide? How can we prevent it from affecting our loved ones and others? And, furthermore, how does the Book of Jonah inform our compassion in such desperate and desolate times?

A remarkable passage shows how far one sage went to preserve his own life—and to prevent suicide:

> The Romans found Rabbi Chanina [ben] Teradyon sitting and occupying himself with the Torah, publicly gathering assemblies, and a scroll of the Law was placed in his bosom. They took hold of him, wrapped him in the Torah scroll, placed bundles of branches around him and set them on fire. They [then] brought tufts of wool, which they had soaked in water, and placed them over his heart, so that he should not expire quickly [elongating this painful death]. . . . His students said to him, ". . . Open your mouth so that the fire will enter into you [and you may die quickly]." [Rabbi Chanina ben Teradyon] replied to them, "Let God who gave [me my soul] take it away, but no one should injure oneself [to hasten one's demise]."[100]

But there is something else of note in this story. Long before modern knowledge about psychiatric illness and suicide, the ancients understood that only those who suffer greatly would consider committing suicide. The following passage demonstrates the sensitivity of the rabbis for those in pain:

> It once happened that when the son of Gordos fled from the school house and his father pointed to his ear [indicating that he would hit him on it], [the child] became frightened of his father, and [went and] destroyed himself in a pit. They [the parents] asked Rabbi Tarfon and he said, "We do not withhold any [burial rites] from him."
>
> . . .
>
> And there was another case when a young child of B'nei Brak broke a bottle and his father pointed to his ear [threatening to hit him on it], and the child became frightened from him and went and destroyed himself in a pit. And they [the parents] went and asked Rabbi Akiva [if the boy could have full burial rites], and he said, "We deny him nothing."[101]

We see here that the rabbis understood that intimidation, humiliation, and abuse lead to inner pain, and that suicide might be a result from such turmoil.

Mental illness is an objective form of suffering. Consider this rabbinic teaching:

> What is the measure of suffering?[102] . . . Rabbi Elazar said, "If a man had a garment woven for him and it is not agreeable to him [does not fit him]." Rava Ze'ira (and some say: Rabbi Shmuel bar Nachmani) disagrees with Rabbi Elazar, saying, "More than this has been said: 'Even if he was to be served hot [wine], and it was served cold; or cold, and it was served hot!' And you require so much?" Mar the son of Ravina said, "Even if his gown got turned inside out." Rava (some say Rav Chisda, others say Rav Yitzchak, and some say it was taught in a *baraita*) said, "Even if he put the hand into his pocket to take out three coins and he fetched only two."[103]

It is impossible to adequately discern the suffering of others. In *halachah*, suicide came to be recognized as something other than a "breach of the law," which has helped us to grapple with the reality of mental illness as something that overtakes the reality of the suffering. While there was the opinion that one who committed suicide is not to be mourned, there have also always been voices encouraging us to cultivate responsibility and compassion[104] for those suffering. Rabbi Yechiel Michel Epstein (1829–1908, Lithuania) writes:

> To summarize: In regard to suicides, we do attribute any circumstance possible to remove them [from the denial of mourning rites]. For example, we attribute the act to anxiety, depression, or insanity; or to the possibility that the deceased might have thought that suicide would save them from transgressing some of the commandments of the Torah; or similar reasons—because it is indeed an improbable thing that a person would commit such an ugly act with a clear mind. Go and learn from Saul the Righteous [Saul the King; I Samuel 31] who fell on his sword in order to prevent the Philistines from tormenting him. Any situation similar to his is considered "under duress."[105]

However, the Book of Jonah also offers some comfort for those who suffer. Uriel Simon[106] astutely notes though that there are three places where the term "sailors" is replaced with the term for "men" in general;[107] and Dr. Erica Brown in her commentary on the Book of Jonah explains that "even though the words are spelled differently, the word[s] for 'sailors' and 'angels' are homophones in Hebrew."[108] The sailors are, in essence, Jonah's protectors, his "angels," though of course he is not aware of this at the time. At the same time, they are all men. For Jonah, this is a dark moment, and his only response is to spare himself from the sense of failing his mission. Yet, the interpretation of the sailors as "angels" allows us to see that Jonah, even in his darkest moments, is protected and guided—even if he himself does not see that. Though he is a prophet, Jonah is not perfect, but anxious, lonely, and prone to depression—but while Jonah rubs up against death multiple times (on the ship, in the fish, fleeing God, under the hot sun, and so on), he is continually granted the gift of life.

Perhaps the lack of any response from Jonah to God's final question (Jonah 4:11) indicates that Jonah's mission has been fulfilled and that he was finally allowed to die. Nonetheless, one might well assume that Jonah had been dying throughout the book, continuously losing his desire for life. Jonah was unable to feel joy in life.

The miracle of humanity is the capacity for compassion with those who suffer—a capacity that we should exercise to the best of our abilities. Only two things will remain after death: our eternal soul and the indirect effects of all we put into the world.[109] As we edge closer to the unyielding grasp of death, we must strive—carefully, wisely, and with all of our might—to cultivate our eternal soul and to put positivity into the world. That, in the end, is all that will last.

CHAPTER 6
The Fish
On the Relationships between God, Humans, and Animals

> *The Eternal provided a huge fish to swallow Jonah; and Jonah remained in the fish's belly three days and three nights.*
> —Jonah 2:1

On the Role of Animals in God's Creation
JONAH'S SOJOURN in the belly of the fish compels us, as readers and thoughtful Jews, to consider:

- As humans, what is our relationship to non-human animals?
- Do humans truly have dominion over Creation—or are they simply more responsible for it than anybody else?

The first chapter of the Book of Genesis presents us with a conundrum: humans are told they "shall rule the fish of the sea, the birds of the sky, the cattle, the whole earth, and all the creeping things that the creep on earth" (Genesis 1:26). In other words, humans have complete dominion over the animal world. This seems to contradict the human obligation to emulate God's ways, which include being "good to all" (Psalm 145:9). How could the consumption of God's creatures be commensurate with the duty to uphold mercy?[110] Are we meant to be vegetarians?

In contrast to the perspective of the Book of Genesis, in the Book of Jonah it appears to be the big fish that has dominion over humanity, or at least over one human. Jonah is swallowed by the fish, but the fish does not kill him, and Jonah lives. Typically, humans go fishing for consumption, for livelihood, and even for sport. Here, the fish does not want the flesh of Jonah's body. Instead, the fish provides enough space in its own body for Jonah to survive.[111] According to the rabbis, the fish in the Book of Jonah is so important that it was already assigned its task during the days of Creation.[112]

Let us consider the significance of the fish in the Book of Jonah. Surely, this is no ordinary creature, but one with a supernatural quality. It is worth asking, do fish have unique status or symbolism in Jewish tradition?

- There are slaughter laws that apply to land animals but not to fish, which are deemed kosher regardless of the manner killed. Jewish law concerning animals fit for consumption states that slaughter must not cause unnecessary pain to land animals, but has no such statements about fish. As reflected in the laws of kosher food, humans seem to feel less empathy toward fish than toward land animals.[113]
- Meat is to be separated from milk in meals, but fish is *parve* ("neutral")—neither meat nor milk. It seems, indeed, that fish in general inhabit a lower position than other animals within Jewish tradition.

However, Judaism generally values animal welfare:

1. Maimonides explained that animals contain within their divinely sourced existence a determined purpose: they are a part of Creation for their own sake.[114]
2. Among the most eccentric and confusing Jewish traditions is the mitzvah of *shiluach haken*, the commandment "to send away the mother bird before taking the eggs or chicks."[115] What religious imperative could require sending away a mother bird only to steal its most prized resource? What pedagogical or ritual function can this possibly serve? *Shiluach haken* is one of the most potent teachings about animal welfare in all of Jewish thought: It does not explicitly teach us to abstain from eating animals or animal products. However, it does teach us to be mindful

of the pain we cause them and to do everything we can to prevent their unnecessary suffering.

3. How we care for and interact with animals is an indicator of our moral fiber. According to Jewish tradition, humans are imbued with a level of knowledge and power not granted to animals. Elevating the human to an existence designated with special rights does not preclude the possibility of some level of obligation toward animals, nor does it call into question the concept of humans as the pinnacle of Creation. In our contemporary perception of the human-animal relationship, there is too much of a proclivity to ignore the concept of *tza'ar ba'alei chayim*—the rabbinic prohibition against inflicting unnecessary "pain upon animals."[116]

4. Another rabbinic source explains that Moses was chosen as the leader and prophet for the Jewish people *because of his consideration for animals.*[117] The prophets and kings of Israel are often portrayed as compassionate shepherds, as is God Godself, such as in the following verse: "The Eternal is my shepherd, I shall not want" (Psalm 23:1). One may not treat an animal merely as profitable property. Instead, we are not even allowed to eat before we have fed the animals we are responsible for.[118]

Though we will never know what the fish symbolized for Jonah, we can look for the fish in our own lives. Was there a time where we were down and someone lifted us up? When we needed a place of refuge and someone sheltered us? When can we serve as the fish, the place of refuge, for someone else who is tossed overboard?

The Garden of Eden, Vegetarianism, and Messianic Dreams

In the Garden of Eden, which was created to house the newly formed beasts and creatures, humans did not consume animals (Genesis 1:29). After the Flood and Noah's construction of the altar, God understood the violent nature of humans and thus permitted meat consumption (Genesis 8:20–9:3) so they would channel their violent nature to kill animals instead of people.[119] While meat was initially allowed only as a sacrifice to God (Genesis 4:4), it later became permitted as a more regular staple of diets outside of sacrificial worship.

A Talmudic parable marks this biblical shift:

> Rav Yehudah stated in the name of Rav: Adam was not permitted meat for purposes of eating, as it is written, "And God said, 'Look, I have given you all the seed-bearing plants on the face of the earth, and every tree that has in it seed-bearing fruit—these are yours to eat'" (Genesis 1:29). "Yours to eat" and all the animals to eat—but the animals are not yours to eat. But when the children of Noah came, [God] permitted them [to eat the animals of the earth], as it is said, "Any small animal that is alive shall be food for you, like green grasses—I give you [them] all" (Genesis 9:3).[120]

Following this reasoning, which can extend to the consumption of fish as well as poultry and meat, two medieval commentators viewed vegetarianism as a Jewish and broadly human ethical ideal. Rabbi Joseph Albo (ca. 1380–ca. 1444, Spain) and Rabbi Isaac Abarbanel both suggested that a diet without meat was a moral lodestar, because slaughter has the potential to manifest humanity's worst traits.[121] Though the Torah gives full permission to consume meat within certain parameters, this allowance does not translate into an *obligation* to consume meat, but rather grants permission to those who desire it. The Torah states, "And you say: 'I shall eat some meat,' for you have the urge to eat meat, you may eat meat whenever you wish" (Deuteronomy 12:20). Meat may be consumed on the basis of desire, but if one finds the action of eating meat physically, spiritually, or ethically repugnant, then one has the choice to abstain. A commentary in the Talmud even interprets this verse from Deuteronomy as "A person should not eat meat unless they have a special craving for it."[122]

We share this beautiful world with a remarkable diversity of life. Once we fully understand that the world was not created for humanity alone—that the mother bird and her egg are precious to

God—and that we are not entitled to consume whatever we wish, we reach a powerful spiritual Torah ideal.

Animals and Other Living Creatures in the Book of Jonah

The animals in the Book of Jonah are remarkable. A big fish could eat a weak man but does not. A small worm and a shade-giving plant (the *kikayon*) impact the emotions of a prophet (Jonah 4:6–11). Upon hearing his city's fate, the king of Nineveh orders not only all human inhabitants but also the city's animals to fast and wear sackcloth (Jonah 3:7–8), biblical signs of mourning and doing *t'shuvah*. Perhaps these details in the narrative best demonstrate the theological view of the "butterfly effect," which states that we are all interconnected in our earthy existence.[123]

In the last verse of the Book of Jonah (4:11), God's final attempt to help Jonah understand the extent of the tragedy that would come with destroying all of Nineveh, God specifies that if the people did not do *t'shuvah*, the consequences would not only come upon the city's sinful human inhabitants, but would also include the moral disaster of the slaughter of innocent animals. Rabbi David Kimchi explains that the animals deserved no punishment and were worthy of God's protection.[124] God loves and has compassion for all creatures and was therefore willing to advocate for these innocent animals and even give the sinful inhabitants of Nineveh, an enemy Assyrian city, a second chance. God wanted to save all the animals and people of Nineveh and teach Jonah that every single plant is important, but Jonah did not understand.

God, in the Book of Jonah, talks to us. If the Creator of the world cares so much, we should as well. Dr. Erica Brown (b. 1966) writes that God even sometimes uses the animals themselves as messengers for God's teachings to us:

> In his commentary on the Book of Jonah, the eighteenth-century German commentator Rabbi David Altschuler (the Metzudat David VeTzion) observes that the animals of Nineveh wore sackcloth not because they were repenting or had any understanding of

personal transformation but because the citizens of Nineveh, when witnessing their animals fasting and wearing sackcloth, would feel more motivated to change themselves. From the cattle of Nineveh to the great fish to small worm in the story of Jonah, we find that animals are vehicles of salvation and not merely convenience for human beings.[125]

I previously mentioned that in chapter 3, the animals in Nineveh will be fasting for the sins of the Ninevites (Jonah 3:6–8). How can animals be forced to fast? This seems cruel. Did the king of Nineveh expect moral transformation from these animals? Perhaps, interpreted uncharitably, this was the king's way of holding God hostage? One Talmudic passage explores this possibility:

> Rabbi Yehoshua ben Levi said: This was a deceitful repentance. What did they do? . . . They placed nursing calves inside and their mothers outside, nursing donkeys inside and the mothers outside; these [the suckling of offspring] were crying from their side [from hunger], and these [the mothers] were crying from their side. They [the people of Nineveh] said [to God]: If You will not have mercy on us, we will not have mercy upon these [animals].[126]

However, we might more generously interpret the animals' fasting as an expression of the deeply interconnected universe in which human and animal fates are intertwined. Bible scholar Theodor Gaster (1906–1992) suggests:

> Animals are part of the "topocosm"—that is, of the aggregate of living beings and inanimate objects which together constitute the corporate entity and "atmosphere" of a place. Hence, in popular belief, they participate in its fate and fortune. It is in this spirit, for instance, that cattle as well as men are victims of the plagues inflicted upon Egypt at the time of the exodus, and that the prophet Joel can declare, when disaster befalls his country, that "the flocks of sheep too are held guilty."[127]

The Book of Jonah reminds us that we are called upon to be a people of holy compassion, whether it is toward other people, living creatures, or the earth. The great sages of the Talmud consider mercy and compassion to be essential characteristics of being Jewish.[128]

Animal welfare is not just a Jewish concern, but a human one as well. The Creation story is the story of *not just Jews*, but of *every creature* that God found worthy of existence. From the lowliest microbe to the most complex being, all gain life from the same holy source. When we forget our divine origins, we forget our core mission: to be a holy person is to consider the plight of those weaker than oneself and to bring succor to the weak and vulnerable. By being compassionate to animals, we both fulfill the mandate of the Torah and become witnesses to the fragility and triumph of humanity.

CHAPTER 7
On the Power of Prayer
Prayer in Times of Distress

> *Jonah prayed to the Eternal his God from the belly of the fish.*
> —Jonah 2:2

The Paths of Jewish Prayer

UP TO THIS POINT in Jonah's journey, we have seen him shirk his prophetic mission and sow havoc with his deeds. But, even now, Jonah knows that not all is beyond repair. When at his lowest, Jonah performs the only action that comes naturally at a moment of deepest distress—he prays.

Prayer, both in the Jewish sense and in the broader cultural lexicon, represents a uniting and mysterious force. Whether done in private or with a group, the act of praying is a powerful statement of devotion to the Divine and to one another. Prayers said in good faith lift spirits and awaken souls. When our spirits are most distraught, prayer provides us with the strength to reorient our hearts—if we allow ourselves to pray with authenticity.[129]

Is Jonah turning to prayer to acknowledge his wrongdoing and seek forgiveness, or is he merely a scared man trying to save his own life, which he endangered himself? In her commentary on the Book of Jonah, Erica Brown writes that Jonah's prayer "had little to do with repentance. Jonah never once expressed contrition. If he was sorry, these words do not appear in the book. If he felt he wronged God or the people of Nineveh, he made no such admission."[130]

Rather than a prayer of remorse or for forgiveness, Jonah's prayer is one of "thanksgiving" (*hoda'ah*).[131] As it says in Jonah 2:10, "But, I, with loud thanksgiving, will sacrifice to You." He prays with gratitude for being saved from the stormy ocean inside the safety of a big fish.

Prayer and Truth

Perhaps the greatest virtue in prayer is truth. A prayer cannot be uttered before the Creator of the world by someone who hides or speaks lies.[132] Those engaged in prayer must believe wholeheartedly in their words and their underlying meaning.

However, a commitment to truth does not start with prayer, but rather with our everyday interactions. Rabbi Eliyahu Dessler (1892–1953), a teacher of Jewish ethics, writes:

> Concerning the attribute of truth, we find in the writings of Rabbeinu Yonah . . . that "one must walk in the ways of God, which are all true, as it is written, 'You shall walk in God's ways' (Deuteronomy 28:9)." The Sages therefore taught that one should be wary of speaking a falsehood even in the most trivial matters. . . . For those who become accustomed to speaking falsehoods in matters that cause them neither benefit nor detriment will eventually come to lie concerning important matters, and they will not be able to speak the truth since they have become accustomed to speaking falsehood.[133]

Once we commit to truth in our everyday interactions, even small talk, we commit to it in all aspects of life. Prayer requires a level of courage and is an exercise in which we do not hide any dimension of our inner lives. If one is looking to prioritize healing and spiritual communication, then authenticity is the only choice. We must be willing to make ourselves vulnerable, to bare our souls and speak our inner truths, which is not always a simple task. As human beings, our vulnerabilities and imperfections are part of our nature, but acknowledging them in prayer brings us closer to God:

> Rabbi Alexandri said: If a commoner uses a broken vessel, it is a disgrace to them. But the Holy One of Blessing uses broken vessels, as it says: "God is close to the brokenhearted" (Psalm 34:19); [and as it says:] "God heals the brokenhearted" (Psalm 147:3).[134]

Prayer helps us to reach deeper layers of inner truths and brings God closer to us. We should feel no embarrassment about our brokenness, because this very brokenness makes humility and tenderness possible.[135] Thankfully, Judaism offers us the spiritual tools to repair our inner lives, such as prayer practices, Jewish meditation, and *hitbod'dut* ("spiritual isolation"). These practices may help us as they did Jonah while he was separated from humanity during his time below the ship's deck, away from the sailors during the storm, while in the big fish, and during his isolation from Nineveh in the final chapter.

How often must we, via prayer, meditation, and/or *hitbod'dut*, make ourselves this vulnerable and exposed before God? Daily? Just in times of crisis? Within the Jewish tradition, thinkers disagree about the nature and frequency needed for prayer to be meaningful. Maimonides thought the Torah requires Jews to pray once a day.[136] Nachmanides disagreed with Maimonides and argued that the Torah requires us to pray only when distressed by events (such as war).[137] Rabbi Joseph Soloveitchik, a twentieth-century scholar of Torah and philosophy, tried to reconcile these views by arguing that both believed that prayers should emerge from "distress" (*tzarah*): Nachmanides prescribed prayer as a response to the brokenness of the outer world, while Maimonides said it should respond to inner brokenness. Rabbi Soloveitchik says:

> Certainly, the Psalmist's cry, *Min hameitzar karati Yah* ("Out of my straits, I have called upon the Lord"; Psalm 118:5) refers to an inner, rather than an externally induced, state of constriction and oppression. Out of this sense of discomfiture prayer emerges. Offered in comfort and security, prayer is a paradox, modern methods of suburban worship and plush synagogues notwithstanding.... Real prayer is derived from loneliness, helplessness, and a sense of dependence. Thus, while Nahmanides dealt only with surface crisis—*tzarot tzibbur*, "public distress," Maimonides regarded all life as a "deep crisis"—a *tzarat yachid* ("private distress").[138]

Maimonides teaches that prayer works to evoke inner change rather than to produce external results. We develop moral rectitude from acts of prayer:

> Certain beliefs are necessary for the removal of injustice or for the acquisition of good morals . . . such as the belief that God responds instantaneously to the cry of someone wronged.[139]

Furthermore, he describes the effect of prayer during times of deep distress:

> The commandment given to us [is] to call upon God in a time of distress. . . . Therefore, we have been commanded to pray to Him, implore Him, and call out before Him in a time of misfortune.[140]

Maimonides thus suggests that the act of prayer in times of distress is not about seeking immediate, magical resolution of a problem, but instead is a way to come closer to our Creator. Maimonides also suggests that prayer cultivates love.[141] Even if prayer in times of distress may primarily be concerned with changing our inner lives rather than changing the outer world, we might still wish for the external circumstances to be altered. However, there is a rabbinic prohibition against praying for what is impossible to change, because it has already happened or been decided. The *Mishnah* says:

> To cry out over that which is past is to utter a prayer in vain. How so? [If a man's] wife is pregnant, and he says, "May it be Your will that my wife give birth to a male," this is a prayer in vain. [Similarly, if] one is coming along the road, and he hears the sound of screaming in the city, [and] he says, "May it be Your will that these [the cries of distress] are not those of my household," this is a prayer in vain.[142]

We may never know Jonah's motivation to pray or the intentions of his prayer. While inside the fish, Jonah is a broken man. Prayer can be a form of light within darkness, a cultivation of hope amid despair, or an act of spiritual rebellion against chaos. We should strive for our prayers to come from a place of sincerity and openness.

The Healing Power of Prayer

Sitting by the sea, we might reflect on what it was like for Noah to come out of the ark and for Jonah to come out of the fish. What is it like to let go of the past and start to shape a new world? Rabbi Hara Person, the chief executive officer of the Central Conference of American Rabbis, has written this poem for Rosh Hashanah, a holiday marking a new beginning:

The sea pushes back off the shore,
yielding to gravity with a sigh,
not a leaving but a letting go,
a retreat into its own deep fullness.
The sun relinquishes its hold on the sky
only to rise once more at daybreak
as the tide rolls back in,
a different kind of letting go,
an unspooling across the expanse.
And we creatures of earth are granted a fresh start,
a chance to gather the debris
and shape a whole new world. . . .[143]

It is at the threshold of the shore where we can feel closest to Creation and new beginnings.

We cannot objectively evaluate how prayer "works" or even whether it does. The effects of praying are felt in our hearts and imprinted on our soul. What we can observe is that prayer has a healing power, because prayer requires that the person praying open up to a sense of both vulnerability and hope. When a person begins to pray, that person believes that God listens. God does not need prayer to be content with Creation, but God cares about prayer because of its power to imbue the human spirit with joy and meaning. We might emerge from individual darkness, as Jonah emerged from the darkness of the belly of the fish, to find wholeness and holiness once again. Through redemption, we can start life anew. There is nothing like the quiet after the storm, the joy and relief of the cessation of chaos. Ibn Ezra explains that the phrase in the Book of Jonah "And the sea was quiet" (Jonah 1:15) is echoed in Psalm 107:30, "They rejoiced when all was quiet."[144] Quiet can bring joy, which in turn can bring growth. We need not be immersed in crisis to pray. Rather, we can stir ourselves each day—with joy, with outrage, with yearning, with anxiety—and awaken ourselves from mere routine to the open and visionary. We do not know that our prayers will be answered, but we can hope that they will at least be heard, if not by God, then by the inner layers of ourselves.

Avivah Zornberg writes, "The enigmas that enrage and sadden Jonah are not riddles to be solved. They remain; God invites Jonah to bear them, even to deepen them, and to allow new perceptions to emerge unbidden. In a word, to stand and pray."[145] When faced with life's problems and paradoxes, sometimes all we can do is stand in prayer.

CHAPTER 8

The World inside the Fish
The Fish and the Dove as Theological Metaphors

The Fish: Depth and Transition

Each day brings fresh challenges—in family, work, culture, and politics—that trick us into thinking that we cannot survive to the next. It can be difficult to step out of this consciousness and hope for something beyond the banal, to yearn for something more substantial in our quotidian experiences. We have to wonder how Jonah might have felt when all the possible challenges he faced coalesced into a singular physical experience: that of being isolated and trapped within the bowels of the fish.

Jonah spent three full days in the bowels of the fish. The *Midrash* lists many other events that occur in the Bible over the course of three days, in addition to Jonah's experience, such as these three experiences:

- Abraham and his son Isaac's walk toward the *akeidah*, the Binding of Isaac, for three days.
- The people of Israel anticipate the divine revelation at Sinai for three days.
- Queen Esther prepares to meet with Achashverosh for three days. [146]

Interestingly, in Jewish tradition, the concept of *chazakah* (which in a technical sense can be defined as "presumption") means that an act done three times becomes a solidified and established custom that has taken on the legal force of a vow, or *neder*.

What was it like for Jonah in the belly of the fish? How did this experience alter his perception of reality? Of humanity? What happened there that changed his perspective on life?

The Malbim (Meir Leibush ben Yehiel Michel Wisser, 1809–1879, Ukraine) suggests that the belly of the fish was like a womb in which Jonah was reborn.[147] Jonah is placed there to reflect, repent, and emerge an entirely new man.

But Jonah does not repent—and yet, he is released.[148] Even after his miraculous rescue, Jonah continues to defy the command of God.[149]

Maimonides explains that there are three steps to repentance: "confession" (*vidui*), "regret for wrongdoing" (*charatah*), and "committing to a new future path" (*kabbalah al he'atid*).[150] In spite of Jonah not undertaking those steps, he is released. This should be encouraging to us. Every year during the High Holy Days, we remind ourselves to commit to be our best selves, but do we ever really complete the spiritual work to get there? Still, even while acknowledging the incomplete nature and the imperfection of our spiritual journeys, we might feel God's closeness and love for us. We learn that when we work to be our best, God accepts us despite our flaws.

Jonah's story is, like our own stories, a story of spiritual incompletion and spiritual imperfection.[151] Perhaps it is his very flight that garners God's attention. It is one thing to run in an era of skepticism when we can neither see nor hear God, but it is quite another to run directly from the voice and command of God. This is perplexing to God. Maybe God perceived Jonah the way a parent perceives their sweet little child lying or rebelling for the first time. The parent feels more curious than angry. Maybe Jonah's soul turns into a research project for God, and the fish becomes God's laboratory.

The biblical text begins by describing God in the third person (*Elohav*), but as he prays Jonah in fact uses the first person (*Elohai*)—indicating that God is not an abstract idea for him, but rather a being that Jonah feels, or at least seeks to be, connected to. Sometimes we need a retreat from the larger world. The fish might function as a laboratory for God, but to Jonah it serves as a sanctuary to where he can retreat to reflect, undergo personal healing, and transform. The fish represents the liminal location between the chaotic storms and the calm of salvation. It is both the place where Jonah is held in transition and a religious space of repentance.

We might think of the fish as Jonah's state of mind. Immersed in the belly of a sea creature, he sees the world through a new lens. He dreams, is lost, searches for salvation, and dives to the bottom of the sea, yearning for a new reality.[152] Rashi argues that Jonah does not actually go into *she'ol* (sometimes understood as a form of "hell"[153]), but that he feels the belly of the fish to be *like* a hell.[154]

The Dove: Hope and Survival

Jonah is not merely a figure within his own story but is also a representative of the entire Jewish people. After all, the literal translation of *yonah* is "dove," a messenger of peace for the world. As Jonah is swallowed and rescued by the fish, so are the Jewish people subsumed and then redeemed. Survival in exile is nothing short of miraculous.[155]

Just as Jonah evaded death, the Jewish people too have miraculously skirted extermination on numerous occasions. The survival of Judaism and the Jews continues to inspire and to offer hope, even in the most dire of circumstances.

CHAPTER 9

Jonah Remained in the Fish's Belly
On Solitary Confinement and Compassion

The Eternal provided a huge fish to swallow Jonah; and Jonah remained in the fish's belly three days and three nights. Jonah prayed to the Eternal his God from the belly of the fish.
—Jonah 2:1

Imprisonment and Isolation

How DOES THE BOOK OF JONAH help us understand imprisonment and isolation from community? Deep within the great fish, Jonah is separated from community, light, and the warmth of the sun.

Prolonged isolation and confinement can lead to serious psychological damage.[156] Yet most courts and legislatures have been unwilling to declare this harsh practice unconstitutional. Do we have no compassion? Solitary confinement, especially for longer than a few weeks or continued indefinitely, is psychological torture and should be considered cruel and unusual punishment. Lack of human contact and sensory deprivation can lead to mental illness or even suicide. When humans are starved of human interaction and companionship, they become unfit for social interaction.[157]

Solitary confinement is an abusive means of control over other human beings, as it slowly erodes its victims' mental identities to the point of destruction.[158] In order to be "safely removed from society," these people are stripped of their basic humanity, becoming instead hazards to themselves. Those who survive the ordeal of open-ended time in solitary confinement leave their situation with prolonged feelings of lethargy and apathy, and they frequently are unable to build new or meaningful relationships with others. Any hope to be rehabilitated into society evaporates during their forced punishment.[159]

According to a study published by the Association of State Corrections and Yale Law School, there are at least eighty thousand inmates in the United States living in isolated and extremely harsh conditions that regularly violate international human rights law.[160] How can this system be allowed to flourish? Several hundred years ago, religious advocates of solitary confinement argued that it provides the opportunity for one to reflect on one's sins and that this would lead to reformation. But today, we should know that being locked alone in a forty-eight-square-foot cell does not lead to the envisioned positive transformation of the soul.[161]

While there may be specific cases where limited isolation of a criminal is needed to protect others, the practice is used far beyond these circumstances. At the least, we should implement isolation time limits, better data collection, and more mental health screening and care in addition to reductions in overcrowding and overall incarceration rates. Inmates should be informed of the length of their solitary confinement and what they can do to increase or decrease that time. There should be a reduction of isolation by using out-of-cell time and a system of progressive housing when transferring prisoners out of solitary confinement and back into the general population.

Solitude and Isolation in Jewish Sources

The present situation brings us back to the Jewish response to punishment. *T'shuvah* ("repentance") is best achieved through positive relationships, not isolation. In a biblical "city of refuge" (*ir miklat*; Numbers 35), the residents (prisoners who unintentionally killed someone) lived with the Levites (who tended to hold leadership roles in their generation). Rehabilitation and growth happen not in isolation, but rather around role models of compassion, spirituality, and good values.

In the Torah, a person who is stricken with *tzara'at* (a Hebrew term understood to be some kind of enigmatic spiritual leprosy) is popularly associated with sinful behavior[162] and is banished from the community completely. Such a person lived a doomed and stunted existence, beleaguered by the pain of separation from community and human contact. Though banishment seems harsh, it is in some ways less punitive than contemporary justice, for even a person with *tzara'at* was allowed to abide just beyond the settlement limits until the skin affliction passed. The belief prevalent today that "prisoners get what they deserve" is counter to what is really needed—compassion and respect for all human beings.

Throughout history, Jewish sages have at times been victims of solitary confinement. In a Talmudic story, seventy-two rabbinic sages are gathered by King Ptolemy before being separated and placed in solitude to translate the Torah into Greek. With God's intervention, all of them produce the exact same translation.[163] The result of this torture is destructive to Torah: The unified interpretation of the Torah into another language might symbolize how confinement destroys the potential for human uniqueness and personal nuance.

While we may embrace limited periods of solitude as a spiritual practice (*hitbod'dut*), extreme forced isolation is not an acceptable punishment. As society debates the efficacy of this practice, the Jewish community must continue to be at the forefront of the struggle against solitary confinement.

A Call for Compassion

In the ending days of his administration, President Barack Obama issued executive orders that moderately curbed some extreme practices of solitary confinement in federal prisons. The president's executive orders on the matter primarily focused on giving juveniles relief from solitary confinement, offering many a second chance. In a 2016 editorial published by the *Washington Post*, President Obama writes:

> The United States is a nation of second chances, but the experience of solitary confinement too often undercuts that second chance. Those who do make it out often have trouble holding down jobs, reuniting with family, and becoming productive members of society. Imagine having served your time and then being unable to hand change over to a customer or look your wife in the eye or hug your children.[164]

As Jews, we are motivated by an existential statement about the human condition made at the beginning of the Torah, when God uttered *lo tov heyot ha'adam l'vado*—"It is not good that the man be alone" (Genesis 2:18).[165] A passage from the Talmud reiterates this point, comparing a life of isolation and lacking meaningful discourse to that of the eternal void: "Either friendship or death."[166] Additionally, modern medicine is now showing the harmful effects of loneliness on our health.[167]

It is not pleasant to be alone, especially inside a fish. It is dark and hopeless, with no one to hear your cries. In solitude, Jonah comes to prayer out of desperation. Perhaps it helped that he was not placed within a cold cell (or an inanimate seashell) but instead within the belly of a living being, right near its present, living, beating heart. But solitary confinement in American prisons does not, and cannot, lead to repentance, but only to prolonged suffering and desperation. Partnership and companionship are part and parcel of a good life.

Jewish values are opposed to the ill-treatment of prisoners, including solitary confinement, no matter their crime. While I would not be so naïve to suggest that individuals who pose a threat to society should not be separated, years-long stints in solitary confinement go beyond rehabilitative corrections and err toward societal sadism.

Showing compassion toward those who may not deserve it is a moral conundrum, and advocating for their basic emotional needs can be a thankless task. Nevertheless, the Jewish mandate to protect the inherent dignity of all human beings, even those who have transgressed the laws of society and morality (e.g., the Ninevites), was as essential to Jonah's prophetic mission as it is for us today. If we mistreat our enemies, we are no better as spiritual beings than they. We might even be ethical cowards or hypocrites, dilettantes in a field that needs prophetic leadership. Solitary confinement is injurious to society.

Jonah, however, seems to prefer solitude (unless this was an outcome of the trauma of his three days confined in the fish). He seems disinterested in engaging with anyone and even keeps his repentance message to the Ninevites to five words (Jonah 3:4). This may be another indication that he wants as little interaction with Nineveh, an enemy city, as possible and that he doesn't even want his message to succeed, perhaps wishing instead for the city's downfall. Jonah eventually settles down to the east of the city (Jonah 4:5) because he finds Nineveh and its inhabitants so distasteful that he can't even reside there. Instead, he sits outside the city, isolating himself completely.

At times, we must remove ourselves from negative forces in order to not be influenced by them. An alternative possible approach, however, is to stand at the city gates (neither fully in nor fully out) by the poor and the sick. In fact, the Talmud says that the Messiah will be found at the city gates, wrapping bandages.[168] As compassion drops in America,[169] we need more than ever to engage and embrace those different from ourselves, rather than retreat into narrow spaces where we are comfortable but ultimately alone.

CHAPTER 10

The Gender of the Fish
A Theology beyond Gender Norms

EMBEDDED IN THE BOOK OF JONAH is a concept that lay dormant for millennia but has contemporary wisdom to impart. The first verse of the book's second chapter says that Jonah was swallowed by a *dag* ("male fish"), but in the next verse, Jonah calls to God from the belly of a *dagah* ("female fish"). What is going on here? Rashi argues that the male fish spat Jonah into the mouth of a female fish.[170] Rather than believing that the fish changes its gender, Rashi offers that perhaps two different fish swallowed Jonah.[171] A more literal read is that there is only one fish that holds different genders at different times.

Did the Book of Jonah provide a precedent for transgender rights and dignity, thousands of years before it became a focus of modern culture?

We do not know the intention of the book's author, but the appearance of masculine and feminine forms in the text might challenge our own gender sensitivities in word usage, especially in referring to God as "He."

As Mary Daly said, "As long as God is male, the male is God."[172] God is not human. God is genderless; God is not male, female, or any other gender. When we limit God to one gender, we limit the ways in which we can think about and experience God. God, as we will explore, exists not within binaries but within the unity of all things, including gender.

Maybe transgender folks can help us to expand the ways we may imagine and experience God.

Those of us who use the traditional liturgy have to own that we may cause damage to others by constantly referring to God in masculine terms, for example, as "Father." We also pray from texts that sexualize God in a heterosexual fashion.[173] While our traditional liturgy certainly has the power to be remarkably moving and trans-formative, it is more accessible to straight and cisgender males than to anyone else. Many of our more traditional communities are not interested in evolving their prayer language. As a result, we are alien-ating, hurting, and excluding countless people searching for God.[174]

When the world was created, so tells us the biblical text of Genesis 1, God crafted the human on the sixth day. This version tells us that man and woman were interconnected and created simultaneously. The second narrative in Genesis 2, however, suggests that man was created first, and then from him, woman was created. While it is cer-tainly true that a plain reading of the first biblical passages of Genesis 1 suggests that the dyad of man and woman was one of the most per-tinent intentions of Creation, a textual analysis of the second version presents another view: identities of gender, sex, race, and ethnicity are not determined by nature but are largely constructed much later by us, the humans, to help us make sense of the world. The Hebrew term *adam* is usually used to describe someone with a male identity. But in the early passages of Genesis, the meaning of the term remains ambiguous. The term *adam* is used to indicate one person. The "human," *adam*, is taken from *adamah*, which simply means "earth," implying that all humans emerged from the universal substance of nature. Though the second version of the story of Creation seems to contradict the first story *prima facie*, it adds a vital dimension to the Creation narrative by emphasizing that all human beings are related to each other through substances found on the Earth: bones, flesh, and blood. While Genesis 1 states that all humans are created equal, Genesis 2 states that while we are all created equal and connected to each other, each of us is needed and unique. Each one of us contrib-utes a singular perspective and voice of prophecy, activism, theology, and spirituality to the human community.

Thus, Adam and Eve (equals, coming from the same earth, being of the same gender and only later to be separated) are not only the first human beings, but also archetypes of humanity as a whole. All of us descend from them, and so we can imagine them containing us all: Adam and Eve as black, brown, and white; gay, bi, queer, and straight; male, non-binary, and female; citizens of the Garden of Eden and stateless refugees from the garden, made from heaven with the sole purpose to inhabit the earth.

The rabbis taught that God has a miraculous capacity for creating all humans as descendants from one and yet, concurrently, each of us as a unique human being:

> When a human being strikes many coins from one mold, they all resemble one another, but the supreme Sovereign of sovereigns, the Holy One of Blessing, fashioned every person in the stamp of the first human, and yet not one of them resembles another. For this reason, every human being is obligated to say, "For my sake, the world was created."[175]

This is not a trivial observation. Shimon Ben Azzai, a Jewish sage who lived in the beginning of the second century CE, taught that "'This is the genealogy of Adam' (Genesis 5:1) is the great principle of the Torah."[176] We understand that a single set of beings contained within them all of our complexity and spiritual DNA. At the same time, the story displays to us that the human dignity of those first people is innate to every subsequent person, regardless of their composition or persuasion.

Those biblical teachings are of the utmost importance for us today. Threats of racism, xenophobia, homophobia, and transphobia prove that humanity is still needlessly looking for reasons to divide itself. However, diversity is not something to push back against in the name of the Bible. The Bible contains an ancient mandate of giving aid to the stranger, giving succor to the weak, and being kind to all. In believing in this mandate, we embrace the notion that all of us were contained in God's Creation. All of us are part of the original plan!

We should make space for diversity so that all of us can flourish. Too often, societies have marked and pushed away anyone who does not fit neatly into their simplified categories. However, today we can bring kindness and justice back into the world. We can embrace the opportunity, and indeed the imperative, to support those who are suffering from marginalization and shaming.

The Book of Jonah, in a brief but most profound way, nods to the complexity of gender. The hero of the story, the fish without a voice or a name, cannot be categorized as either male or female. Its gender refuses categorization. What matters most is that it is a nurturing, safe space of refuge. That is what God asks of all of us to provide—nurturing, safe spaces of refuge—each of us in our own feminine, non-binary, or masculine way.

CHAPTER 11

Jonah Is Saved
On Godly Justice

> *God commanded the fish, and it spewed Jonah out upon dry land.*
> —Jonah 2:11

On Noah, Abraham, and Jonah:
Three Moments of Impending Mass Destruction

As WE HAVE SEEN so far on our journey with the idiosyncratic prophet, Jonah is a character to whom we can all relate, particularly when we compare him to other biblical figures. Think of Noah (Genesis 6–8), quietly packing the ark, while the rest of the world and all life are destroyed.[177] Think of Abraham: in his willingness to sacrifice his own son, he seems to be entirely emotionally remote (Genesis 22). We cannot identify with them!

Jonah, on the other hand, runs from God. We all do that. We understand this reaction.

However, in a moment of despair, Jonah suddenly seems to remember that God not only places great demands on us, but also rescues us from danger. Perhaps Jonah recalls the moment when, at the initial formation of the Jewish people, we were saved from the Egyptian soldiers and the dangerous waters of the splitting sea. Rabbi Steven Bob, a contemporary American rabbi, says about the use of the terms *yam* ("sea"; Jonah 2:4) and *yabashah* ("dry land"; Jonah 2:11):

> In three places—Exodus 14:16, Exodus 14:22, and Nehemiah 9:11—the text uses these words [*yam* and *yabashah*] to describe the division of the Reed Sea and the saving of the Israelites from the Egyptians. Jonah's use of the phrase hints at his hope that God save this ship from the storm by returning it to dry land, as God saved the Israelites from the Egyptians.[178]

Though the splitting of the sea was witnessed by hundreds of thousands while Jonah experienced a private miracle, there exists a parallel between these two stories.

The belly of the fish, for Jonah, is like the ark for Noah. In the story of Noah, it rained for "forty days *and forty nights*" (Genesis 7:12), and in the Book of Jonah, Jonah is in the belly of the fish for "three days and *three nights*" (Jonah 2:1). Both stories tell us about a period of forty days before destruction (Genesis 7:17, 7:23; Jonah 3:4). Animals play significant roles in the plots of both stories (Genesis 7:21; Jonah 3:7–8). Both Noah and Jonah appear to be harsh judges of others. Both appear to be oblivious: Noah gets drunk in the new world, while Jonah goes to sleep amid the storm.[179]

However, the story of Jonah is different from that of Noah in that Jonah was asked to give the people of Nineveh a chance to redeem themselves, whereas we do not know whether Noah was instructed to warn his contemporaries of the Flood, nor whether he does so. In the Book of Jonah, Jonah delivers five words that cause tens of thousands of people to repent (Jonah 3:4), while Noah utters nothing as God destroys the world and everything outside the ark. Maybe the people drowned in the Flood were so wicked that they deserved no redemption, while those of Nineveh were decent people who had erred and deserved another chance. Alternatively, the Book of Jonah might be read as a *tikkun* (a "repair") for the Noah story: Noah (and God?) missed an opportunity to help people repent. Not wanting to repeat that elision, God sends the prophet Jonah on a different mission altogether: not to save only the righteous, but to help the sinners repent.

Judy Klitsner, a contemporary Bible scholar living in Israel, contrasts the two stories:

> In general, Noah's story reverses that of Jonah in its approach to destruction. In the Noah narrative, humanity's annihilation was neither negotiable nor avoidable; God and His prophet were united in viewing death as inevitable. The inverted details of the Book of Jonah will lead us away from destruction as a narrative

necessity. They will point instead toward a more generous view of humanity adopted by God and by humanity itself.[180]

The generation of Noah did not repent and was thus destroyed. The people of Nineveh, on the other hand, *do* repent and are thus saved. It's for this reason that Klitsner astutely suggests that "the Book of Jonah serves as a subversive sequel to the story of Noah."[181]

In the story of Noah the Righteous, only the righteous and his family survive. In the Book of Jonah, on the other hand, the prophet's life is endangered in order to save an entire city of sinners. Klitsner writes:

> In the Flood narrative, the prophet floated safely in his boat as the world around him drowned. In the Book of Jonah, the world floats as the prophet faces death by drowning. Furthermore, in an ironic narrative twist, the world is now more moral and more compassionate than the prophet. Rather than leaving the doomed to die at sea—as Noah did with his contemporaries—the boat's inhabitants strive mightily to keep their fellow human being dry and safe.[182]

The sailors in the Book of Jonah display the kind of compassion and mercy we would consider righteous today. Oddly enough, though, it is Noah who is remembered as "the Righteous." A *midrash* defends him, arguing that he, indeed, did forewarn the people.[183]

Just as different as Noah and Jonah are from one another, God also reveals Godself very differently in the story of Noah than in the Book of Jonah. Whereas God gives no instruction to Noah to call upon the people to repent, God cares about the masses and their repentance in the Book of Jonah. The Book of Jonah tells the story of the repentance of an entire city, the repentance of a prophet, and maybe also of God's own repentance.

Erica Brown writes about the surprising connection between Jonah and his biblical antecedent, Noah:

> The greatest common denominator in both narratives is the water. . . . Water is everywhere. Water involves great risk; the sea is unpredictable and indifferent to human life. It is vast. It is calming. It is treacherous. Its surface can betray its depths and its dangers. Jonah

and Noah are both watery tales, and their maritime flavor forces a natural comparison between these two protagonists and the landscape that shaped them: one was almost lost to water and another redeemed through it. Jonah put others at peril when he boarded a ship. Noah preserved the remnants of a lost world when he boarded his. Both stories involve animals: those that save and those that are saved. Both involve a background of nameless human beings: those who are inexpressibly good and those who are irredeemably wicked.[184]

When the deluge ends, Noah releases a dove (Genesis 8:8–9), but this dove does not find redemption on its first flight. Only the second time does it return with a branch (Genesis 8:10–11). Like Noah's dove, Jonah needs a second try to bring redemption to the land of Nineveh. Both yonahs (Noah's "dove" and Jonah, the "dove") are called upon to be messengers of peace. It takes both of them a few tries to achieve their peace message.

When comparing Jonah and Abraham and their respective senses of justice, the two stories stand in even greater contradiction. Whereas Abraham pleads with a God who seems adamant on destroying a wicked city, Jonah urges for the destruction of a city that God seems adamant on saving. Whereas Abraham argues, "Must not the Judge of all the earth do justly [to the innocent righteous living in Sodom and Gomorrah]?" (Genesis 18:25), Jonah invokes justice to argue for the extinction of the entire city of Nineveh. Both men challenge God in the name of justice, but while Abraham warns that righteous people might get killed (Genesis 18:23–25), Jonah worries that sinners might be saved. And, in contrast to the God of Genesis, the God of the Book of Jonah promotes mercy.[185]

In the belly of the fish, however, Jonah himself is saved through God's mercy. He is taught an important lesson on compassion and mercy and is given a new chance for life.

CHAPTER 12

God's Wrath
The Ethics of Compassion

YONAH BEN AMITAI (Jonah, a "person of truth") is just too committed to truth. He prioritizes principled truth over all other values.
In Jewish thought, however, truth alone never outweighs mercy.
Preserving peace, saving a life, and protecting another's dignity
outweigh truth, albeit cautiously and with trepidation. Jonah is so
committed to truth that he even rebukes God for not being truth-
ful enough. If God were primarily concerned with truth, then God
would destroy Nineveh for its past wickedness and expected future
evil (when their repentance fades away). Instead, God seemingly prioritizes compassion over truth.

Jonah shows no interest in imitating God in this regard. He does
not value the peace covenant of the rainbow that God entered with
us after Noah's Flood. The seven colors of the rainbow represent the
seven days of Creation—and the nuances of truth! But Jonah wishes
to see the world in black and white. The story of Noah, with the covenant of the rainbow, promises a world without mass destruction.
Jonah's story ends with the symbol of a withering plant, representing
a world lacking compassion and mercy. Only in a world full of mercy
and compassion will we endure! Only in such a world will we fulfill
the plan of God's Creation.

It is not entirely clear if it was ever truly God's plan to destroy
Nineveh. Both in the story of Abraham (Genesis 19:25, 19:29) and
in the story of Jonah (Jonah 3:4), the destruction of the wicked city
is referred to as an "overturning," but Rashi notes that this verb can
mean "transform" rather than "destroy."[186] In the end, Nineveh
was not destroyed but overturned and transformed. Interestingly,

the people of Nineveh seem to have believed in the power of repentance and in God's compassion from the beginning—in spite of the story of Sodom and Gomorrah, in which God dooms a wicked city and destroys it without giving any second chances at all. Maybe the Ninevites were oblivious of this past.

In spite of Abraham's pleadings, God decides to destroy the city of Sodom because its citizens lack mercy and compassion. In fact, the Sodomites actually punished anyone who showed compassion! One rabbinic teaching shares that the final straw for God was when the people of Sodom discovered a young girl feeding a starving beggar, and they smeared honey all over her and tied her to the city wall until she died from bee stings.[187]

The world in which Noah lives was destroyed because of its violent nature. So God said to Noah, "The end of all flesh has come [to mind] before Me, because the earth is full of violence on their account; look, now—I am going to wipe them off the earth" (Genesis 6:13). The rabbis emphasize that this first version of humankind was destroyed owing to their theft and "violence" (*chamas*).[188] The world was flooded as punishment for its violence.

So, why does God begin to pay attention to the city of Nineveh? After all, people do harmful things all over the world. Jonah 1:2 says, "Their wickedness has come before Me." What was the sin to be found in Nineveh? According to Rabbi David Kimchi, like the first people, Nineveh's crime was "violence" (*chamas*) as well.[189]

In each of the stories, it is violence that angers God. However, in the story of Jonah, God reaches out to the violent sinners and calls for their repentance! In the Book of Jonah, God wants to be merciful—God wants to forgive.

Abarbanel even claims that the people of Nineveh never fully repent of their false faith, but remain idolaters. They merely change their wicked ways, which is sufficient for God, who values the ethical more than the theological.[190] Abarbanel also suggests that Jonah, too, is not troubled by Nineveh's idolatry. Instead, Jonah fears that the Ninevites, once they survive God's judgment, might rise up and kill the Israelites. According to Abarbanel, Jonah wishes to die because he does not want to witness his own people suffering and perishing. Yet, Jonah seems unconcerned with the suffering of the Ninevites. His compassion is limited to the people he identifies with. Sadly, this kind of limited compassion is not unusual. Throughout history, we have seen people display enormous compassion for "their own" while acting cruelly or indifferent toward "the other."

It is so easy for us to judge Jonah for his lack of compassion and mercy for those different from him and his own people. However, the rabbis teach that we should not judge anyone until we have been in their place.[191] When we read the Book of Jonah on Yom Kippur, we are reminded of this teaching: we should not judge Jonah, just as we should not judge the prayer of those in our pews, the voices of the cantor and choir, the sermon of the rabbi, or the authenticity of our family's commitment. Would we really do any better than Jonah if asked to speak truth to 120,000 people in a city far more powerful than our own, where we lack all legal rights and protections and carry no social capital?

It is easy to scream and blame others (politicians, neighbors, detractors). However, instead of blaming others, we need to look inward and ask if we are doing enough ourselves. It is not an easy question to ask. We may prefer to blame others instead. We may prefer to point to our own suffering instead of examining our own actions.[192] We may prefer to judge others in order to avoid judging ourselves.[193] We are not allowed to do that. Analyze and learn, we must. But proclaim ourselves superior to Jonah, we must not. Instead, God calls us to be merciful and look on others with compassion.

CHAPTER 13

Nineveh Fasts
The Book of Jonah as a Reading on the Day of Repentance

AT THIS POINT in our journey with Jonah, we have seen his travails, his anxieties, his escape from duty, and his merciless sense of justice. He is a prophet who does not live up to God's expectations, nor does he live up to ours. However, rather than disregarding the Book of Jonah for these reasons, the rabbis proposed the opposite: they insisted that the book be read on Yom Kippur, the holiest and most solemn date on the Hebrew calendar.[194]

The liturgical context of the fast day Yom Kippur reveals new insights in the theological messages of the Book of Jonah. The theology of the Day of Atonement speaks about recognizing human failure, and specifically our collective inability to raise ourselves above pettiness and evil. The High Holy Day season—and Yom Kippur in particular—instills in us the knowledge that we have multiple opportunities for spiritual growth.

The Book of Jonah says about fasting: "The people of Nineveh believed God. They proclaimed a fast, and great and small alike put on sackcloth" (Jonah 3:5). The citizens of Nineveh also engage in immediate and complete repentance, just as it is prescribed for Yom Kippur: "They shall be covered with sackcloth . . . and shall cry mightily to God. . . . Who knows but that God may turn and relent? God may turn back from wrath, so that we do not perish" (Jonah 3:8–9). The repentance of the Ninevites is so sincere that God immediately accepts it: "God saw what they did, how they were turning back from their evil ways. And God renounced the planned punishment, and did not carry it out" (Jonah 3:10).

Commentator Abraham Ibn Ezra also argues that the repentance of the Ninevites is genuine:

> In the earliest days they [the Ninevites] had been God-fearing, and it was only recently, in the days of Jonah, that they started to do evil. If they had not been God-fearing people, God would not have sent his prophet to them. We see that they did complete, unparalleled repentance. As a proof, it [the Book of Jonah] does not say that they smashed altars or idols. From this we learn that they had not been idol worshipers.[195]

Nonetheless, Jonah flees from his mission, some suggest, precisely because he does not believe that the repentance of the Ninevites is sincere. Abarbanel, for example, writes:

> The truth of the matter is that Jonah regretted fleeing God and promised in his heart to fulfill God's command [to call on] Nineveh. But he was comforted in his realizing that the people of Nineveh were worshipers of nothingness. Even if they did t'shuvah because of his call, they would not be steadfast in their repentance—after a few days, they would leave righteousness behind again and return to [being] evil.[196]

Fasting, contrition, and repentance—those motifs of the Book of Jonah resonate with the theology of Yom Kippur. The people of Nineveh fast and repent, and God accepts their repentance. The text suggests that if we seek God's forgiveness, we should follow the actions of Nineveh. If we fast, repent, and accept our human imperfection, we will receive salvation from an infinitely forgiving God.

During the High Holy Days, Jews are to change themselves—to return to God—using three sets of actions:

- *T'shuvah* ("repentance")—the process of self-transformative, inner reflective work to improve ourselves.
- *T'filah* ("prayer")—the process of translating that renewed self into intentional, sacred speech and loving, sacred relationships.
- *Tzedakah* ("doing justice")—the process of acting consistently upon our commitments to kindness, justice, and giving back to the world.

Human perfection is impossible. Though human beings can possess godly characteristics, we are unable to reach the level of the perfect Divinity—and also Jonah falls short. Human beings, even prophets, stray from the path of righteousness, but their moral mandates do not fade away. God waits for us to follow our call to redemption. Each of us might resemble Jonah a bit; we might be hiding from our responsibilities, we might feel anxious, angry, or confused. But we, too, are allowed to reengage. The Book of Jonah reminds us that the spiritual energy of *rachamim* ("loving mercy") overpowers the energy of *din* ("moral judgment and punishment"). Mercy outweighs punishment both when executed by God and when carried out by us toward others or ourselves.[197] As Yom Kippur comes to an end, we may still be unsure of our own virtue. We may have humbly questioned our deeds and our intentions. However, we can be sure that God is still the God of love, compassion, and mercy.

When we read the Book of Jonah on Yom Kippur, we learn that God has the capacity to forgive people who embrace abject evil, and so we also focus on finding forgiveness in our own hearts. We reexamine our own ways and perspectives.

Still, this kind of self-examination, intention, and active commitment is not easy to pursue. Jonah himself is an example of someone who fails to do so. Instead, he is livid about God's mercy toward Nineveh (Jonah 4:1–4). Jonah is upset that God did not destroy Nineveh. The journey of Jonah points to the gap between our human behavioral limitations and the ethical ideals God calls us to. This type of journey exemplifies a constant struggle consistently explored within Jewish thought. Rabbi Meir Simcha of Dvinsk (1843–1926, Lithuania) argues that whereas before the biblical sin of the Golden Calf (Exodus 32) we might have been allowed to judge others for their ethical shortcomings, we are now called to focus primarily on our own flaws rather than the faults of others. We must use our spiritual energy for introspection and to improve ourselves. He wonders whether there may be some people among us already righteous enough to judge others, but he concludes that such spiritually elevated individuals are few and far between.

There are times when we must step away from introspection and take up a different and much more active role. The Book of Jonah is read on Yom Kippur precisely because Yom Kippur is a day to awaken from our moral slumber—but also a day reminding us that ethical awakening has to be demonstrated in our deeds and in our continuous spiritual resistance against the evil lurking in our societies. Rabbi Abraham Joshua Heschel writes:

> To us a single act of injustice—cheating in business, exploitation of the poor—is slight; to the prophets, a disaster. To us injustice is injurious to the welfare of the people; to the prophets it is a deathblow to existence: to us, an episode; to them, a catastrophe, a threat to the world.[198]

The path to universal redemption is not solely a return to God but also a return to the path of the just. Invoking the Holocaust, the atomic bombings of Hiroshima and Nagasaki, and the failure of American Jews to care about the casualties in Vietnam, Rabbi Heschel asks, "Jonah is running to Tarshish, while Nineveh is tottering on the brink. Are we not all guilty of Jonah's failure?"[199]

Active commitment without self-reflection and intention is empty. Self-reflection and intention without active commitment are empty, too. When we see the world burning, we are not allowed to stand idly by. On Yom Kippur, we reaffirm our commitment to protect the dignity of life. However, we should renew this commitment every day of our lives. Jonah, in a moment of weakness, flees from his responsibility. Most of us would also be challenged by the responsibility to save countless souls. Most of us would flee not because of cowardice but because we feel overwhelmed and unprepared. Listening to the story of Jonah, we learn that we cannot wait for the day when we conveniently feel ready. We have to act when we are called upon.

CHAPTER 14

God Calls Upon Us
The Human Reluctance to Change

Judaism values equilibrium—achieving a happy medium between base human instinct and what is divinely endowed. Perhaps most vital to achieve, from a Jewish perspective, is the balance between our human "striving" (*hishtadlut*) for more and the "trust" (*bitachon*) in God's care and foresight. Establishing equilibrium between our human instincts and divinely inspired ethics is the greatest marker of internal evolution. How far do we go to satisfy our own needs and wishes? How much energy do we invest in the refinement of our souls? Repentance reflects our desire for holiness. It is the necessary basis for a humanity that is a force of healing rather than hurting, building rather than destroying, and contributing rather than diminishing. When we "return" (*shuv*) to our "divine essence" (*tzelem Elohim*), our souls remember their heavenly origin and reveal the full beauty of humanity.

Does Jonah develop these qualities? Does he develop trust in God? Does he prioritize God's ethics over his own needs and worldview?

Jonah's task is difficult to fulfill. The task requires Jonah to calmly respond to God's call. It requires him to take care of a people he fears and to seek risks he prefers to avoid. It is difficult for Jonah to stay on top of these challenges, especially those that conflict with his worldview. In her analysis of the prophet's life and deeds, Erica Brown observes:

> The world around Jonah is in constant flux. A group of sailors became a group of believers. A city and its king transformed themselves. A tree grew and died overnight. Everything and everyone changed, including God—but the prophet did not change. For this reason, we have no idea what happened to Jonah when the words written about him end.[200]

External change is often experienced as loss. Joseph Campbell (1904–1987, American literary scholar and mythologist) writes, "We must be willing to let go of the life we've planned, so as to have the life that is waiting for us."[201] When we are no longer willing or able to evolve, we may, like Jonah, begin to see death as the only alternative to the ongoing effort of adjusting to change.[202] Intentionally changing our worldviews, plans, and ethics is not easy. It requires the full expansion, depth, and conscience of our true souls as we move ourselves further.

Rabbi Abraham Isaac HaKohen Kook writes:

> The greater the soul, the more it must struggle in order to find itself; the more the depths of the human soul are hidden from the conscious mind. One must have extended solitude and *hitbodedut* [spiritual isolation in self-reflective prayer], examining ideas, deepening thoughts, and expanding the mind, until finally the soul will truly reveal itself, unveiling some of the splendor of its brilliant inner light.[203]

The role of a prophet—and of any other human—is to hold on to one's own deep expansive soul and the consciousness of both the human spirit and the divine direction. This becomes difficult when the future is unknown and elusive. John Dewey (1859–1952, American education and social reformer) writes that humanity's obsessive longing for certainty leads to destructive thoughts and behaviors:

> In morals a hankering for certainty, born of timidity and nourished by love of authoritative prestige, has led to the idea that absence of immutably fixed and universally applicable ready-made principles is equivalent to moral chaos. . . . [There is] another manifestation of the desire to escape the strain of the actual moral situation, its genuine uncertainty of possibilities and consequences. We are confronted with another case of the all too human love of certainty, a case of the wish for an intellectual patent issued by authority.[204]

The desire to avoid change is human, but perilous. Refusal to adapt to change leads to the myopic perspective that the future is merely a predictable reflection of the past. We certainly need reprieve from our current pressures to reflect calmly on our past and, at times, take a break from the present. At the same time, however, we must turn our eye toward tomorrow and prepare to change. Otherwise, the problems of the present will not be solved in the future.

Perhaps the only place where Jonah feels safe is within the great leviathan, a refuge from the chaos. Only there, in a place void of change and disturbances, does Jonah find the space for deep and conscious prayer; only there does he take care of his soul.

The theory of change that emerges from the story of Jonah is maybe the most fascinating part of the book. Erica Brown contrasts the captain and the king with Jonah, writing:

> The captain and the king serve as Jonah's foils; their behavior was meant to communicate to Jonah that his was flawed. . . . [The] captain and the king [highlight] the possibility of change on behalf of another—in this instance, God—because of their own change. They could not control God. They could only control their own actions, and so were determined to do just that. Once they controlled their actions and moved toward transformation, they created a ground that was fertile for shared change. Jonah, on the other hand . . . swam or walked away from the possibility of redemption. But his surety was not at all what God wanted. God was more satisfied with a humility that prompted action than a certainty that prompted inaction.[205]

We are not allowed to celebrate stagnation. We must celebrate history's indefinability and power to influence our hearts and minds so that we can learn from it. Supreme Court Justice Oliver Wendell Holmes (1841–1935) writes, "A page of history is worth a volume of logic."[206]

There is a great tension between learning from history and being fully present in the moment. Indeed, history often makes us more conscious of potential risks, for better and worse. However, while leadership certainly requires caution, it also requires risk-taking.

But the scariest endeavor is not external—changing the world— but internal—working to change ourselves. This is the task that demands the greatest risk-taking propensity. The sailors and the people of Nineveh are able to quickly evolve, in stark contrast to Jonah's initial reluctance to change. They immediately respond to the threats posed before them, whereas Jonah flees.

In the Book of Jonah, God and the world change much faster than the prophet can grasp. Rabbi Abraham Joshua Heschel writes:

> God's change of mind displeased Jonah exceedingly. He had proclaimed the doom of Nineveh with a certainty, to the point of fixing the time, as an inexorable decree without qualification. But what transpired only proved the word of God was neither firm nor reliable. To a prophet who stakes his life on the reliability and infallibility of the word of God, such realization leads to despair. "O Lord, take my life from me, I beseech Thee, for it is better for me to die than to live" [Jonah 4:3] was his prayer.[207]

Perhaps the biggest change we can make in our own lives is to become ready to change. The ever-changing world we live in requires us to asses our own needs and the needs of others every day anew. In order to truly take care of our souls and support others, we have to change—constantly. Only then are we able to give back. That is what it means to take care of our souls.

CHAPTER 15

Jonah's Hatred for the Stranger
On Tribalism, Ethnocentrism, and Fundamentalism in a Pluralistic World

> *I am a Hebrew.*
> —Jonah 1:9

WITH HIS FIRST LINE in the book, Jonah wants to make clear to the gentiles around him that he is first and foremost Jewish. While it is wonderful to be proud of one's identity, it is also worth examining the limits of particularism.

Is the Book of Jonah—and the character of Jonah himself—based around an ethnocentric vision of the world? Does Jonah only care about Jewish survival? Is that why he has no interest in the redemption of the citizens of Nineveh? Is that why he is more preoccupied with absolute "justice" (*din*) than "loving-kindness" (*chesed*)?

By today's standards, if Jonah truly did wish for the mass destruction of a foreign people for religious reasons, he would be considered a *fundamentalist*.[208] Fundamentalism is the most noxious disease in faith communities wrought with demands to silence or to suspend one's own held moral intuition, and instead to submit to another's authority or their authoritative interpretation of a multilayered religious text. When encountering those who hold onto stubborn and harmful dogma, run! Once you think you are truly safe, run even faster. If your average contemporary citizen was to meet someone like Jonah today, he or she should run as well. Fundamentalists despise everyone who is different from them, and Jonah truly despises the Ninevites. And yet, the people of Nineveh, whom Jonah hates so much, become a model for repentance.

At times, we might find ourselves quite similar to Jonah: tribal, parochial, and prejudiced. In our shortsighted wishes to appease the immediate needs of our own communities, we ignore the needs of others.

The question of how to balance religious pride with universal care is not only a religious question. It is a question for society at large, even in a secular state. President Barack Obama writes:

> If we Americans are individualistic at heart, if we instinctively chafe against a past of tribal allegiances, traditions, customs, and cases, it would be a mistake to assume that this is all we are. Our individualism has always been bound by a set of communal values, the glue upon which every healthy society depends. . . . In every society (and in every individual), these twin strands—the individualistic and the communal, autonomy and solidarity—are in tension, and it has been one of the blessings of America that the circumstances of our nation's birth allowed us to negotiate these tensions better than most.[209]

We face the challenge to balance the familiar and known with the other and foreign. Connections to other faith communities, for example, provide gratifications that Jewish communities rarely actualize. However, when we form connections with other faith communities, we begin to learn from each other; we enrich and inspire the lives of the others. In a *midrash*, the rabbis teach about the role of "borrowing from one another" in Creation:

> The day borrows from the night, and the night from the day.
> The moon borrows from the stars, and the stars from the moon. . . .
> Thus it is also with human beings, with a single difference: all these others borrow without ending up in court.[210]

Day does not end discreetly when night begins. Rather, day and night learn from one another; they become a little like each other. Their essences are too intertwined to ever be radically separate. Likewise, the known and the foreign are also interdependent; the two perspectives can and must "borrow from one another."

We are commanded to love our neighbor only once in the Torah, yet we are commanded by the Torah thirty-six times to love and protect a stranger—something utterly more difficult. In the challenge of building such distant relationships, we can find opportunities for change and growth. The familiar determines who we are, the foreign who we might become. The tribal evokes nostalgic memory, while the universal inspires the visionary dream. Rabbi Jonathan Sacks teaches that neither tribalism nor universalism by themselves can sustain the world. While we should love and cherish our unique communities, we also should value and engage with foreign communities and individuals. We should insist that our own communities "borrow" from others. Tribalism, at its best, solidifies community, language, identity, and kindness to "one's own." Universalism, at its best, solidifies interconnection, diversity amid unity, and justice.

Achieving balance requires reverence for the vastness and complexity of the world around us. We must be empowered to engage but at the same time must be aware of our limitations. Our community leadership must model both courage and humility.

A *midrash* on the first chapter of Genesis inspires my own spiritual practice of balancing the familiar with the foreign:

> God gathered the dust [of the first human] from the four corners of the world—red, black, white, and green. . . . Why from the four corners of the earth? . . . Every place we walk, from there we were created and from there we will return.[211]

Though all humans are different, we all belong everywhere. All humans are made up of the same cosmic material and thus share equal dignity. On the other hand, each of us is unique. My own particularism is informed by my relationships and work within my own communities, and I draw on this particularism when I venture beyond their borders (both physical and virtual). I try to use the closeness I feel with God and my own community to make this entire world a smaller and safer place. When I work on complex social change projects, I carry the lights of spiritual intimacy with me. I often feel isolated in activism work. Partners often do not meet their commitments, while opponents often engage in unfair personal attacks. At those times, I try to remember that God is with us. I strive to find the internal and external light that can expel the rampant darkness. Being spiritually prepared allows us to engage in face-to-face conversations and also the vastly more complex and diverse discourse of shared conversations.

Unity of Religions?

Many years ago, at an interfaith gathering in Davos, I witnessed a faith leader stand up and claim that "we are all brothers and sisters, since our faiths are really the same." I recall feeling shocked by the simplicity of that concept. That type of unity can be terrifying. God is not simple, and religion is not meant to be a panacea. True faith and redemption are found in the details of our lives, not in abstract mantras. Not only do we not want to conflate different traditions and value systems, but the need to rationalize the value of every worldview is dangerous. The universalist impulse to render religion essentially uniform may make us feel warm on the inside, but it is devoid of nuance and inherently false.

Anyone moderately familiar with comparative religions knows there are core differences between all faiths, even beyond theological doctrine. For example, Islam and Judaism prohibit eating pork, while in some Christian cultures a pork meal is integral to their holidays. Islam bans alcohol, unlike Judaism and Christianity, which incorporate wine into religious rituals. Present-day Judaism and mainstream Christianity practice monogamy exclusively, but Islam has allowanced polygamy. Most Christian sects have a tradition of religious iconography, while in Islam it is forbidden.[212] If we questioned the status of women within religion, it is doubtful that a consensus could be derived even within individual religions.

Many atheists dismiss "religion" as if it were one entity. However, a more sophisticated approach requires that we contend with each religion and its claims separately. Religions have much in common, and we should come together and learn from each other. That said, we cannot pretend that our truths are identical. Rabbi Lord Jonathan Sacks writes:

> There is a fundamental difference between the end-of-days peace of religious unity and the historical peace of compromise and coexistence. The attempt to force the former can sometimes be the most formidable enemy of the latter. . . . Universalism must be balanced with a new respect for the local, the particular, the unique."[213]

He continues:

> My argument is far more fundamental, namely that universalism is an inadequate response to tribalism, and no less dangerous. It leads to the belief—superficially compelling but quite false—that there is only one truth about the essentials of the human condition. . . . God may at times be found in the human other, the one not like us. Biblical monotheism is not the idea that there is one God and therefore one gateway to His presence. To the contrary, it is the idea that the unity of God is to be found in the diversity of creation.[214]

History has proved what Sacks claims: people who wish to create a universal religion frequently resort to suppression.

- Pharaoh Akenhaten (reigned ca. 1352–1336 BCE) created a religion dedicated to a single deity, the sun disk Aten, but he also spent vast sums building a new city to his new religion and punished those who maintained old beliefs. When he died, his monotheistic experiment was abandoned.
- The founding of Islam was followed by centuries of warfare (spiritual and otherwise) against Christianity, as well as within nations with Islamic rulers.
- From 1096 to 1291, the Christian Crusades sought to take Jerusalem and other areas of the Middle East back from Muslim control. Participants were promised that their sins would be forgiven in exchange for fighting. While

> initially Jerusalem and Mediterranean ports were taken,
> all of the territories were ultimately regained by Muslim
> rulers; we continue to feel the effects of this legacy today.[215]

The best approach, then, is one of coexistence. One interesting case in point involves a Muslim ruler and a majority Hindu population, as unlikely a pairing as can be imagined: Islam is monotheistic and forbids religious imagery, while Hinduism is polytheistic and embraces religious imagery. Islam adheres to the doctrine of an individual soul, while in Hinduism there is belief in reincarnation, which embraces a reverence for animals, which are seen as carriers of the reincarnated spirits of people. Akbar the Great, who ruled India from 1556 to 1605, expanded the Muslim Mughal Empire. He participated in festivals of other religions, married several Hindu princesses, abolished a special tax on Hindus, and did not press for the conversion of Hindus. Later, he built a temple in which he received Hindu, Zoroastrian, and other religious scholars, allowed Christians to build churches, and increased respect for Hinduism by discouraging the slaughter of cattle. At some point, he attempted to create a syncretic religious system that incorporated elements from Islam, Hinduism, and other religious beliefs.[216] The example of Akbar the Great teaches us that the best religious policy might be to appreciate the good points of all religions, while not pretending that a universal religion can be created or imposed on all. In the tumultuous twentieth century, Mohandas Gandhi was the quintessential spokesman for religious tolerance, even though he could not prevent the creation of India and Pakistan as separate Hindu and Islamic states. He rejected the idea that everyone should belong to the same religion. "My effort should never be to undermine another's faith," he said, "but to make him a better follower of his own faith."[217]

Jonah serves as a reminder for us of what happens when we do not follow God's call to care for all beings. Yet, as Erica Brown notes, "the Book of Jonah is the only biblical book to end on a question, perhaps reflecting the ambivalence of Jonah himself and his mission."[218] As

Jonah was given multiple chances to evolve from his narrow theology, so is each of us given multiple chances to cultivate elevated spiritual consciousness and understanding of the interconnectivity of all life.

We must be tolerant of other religions, surely. We need to collaborate and learn from one another. But we should do so in a way that honors and dignifies others' beliefs, rather than merely eliding difference. As religious, or spiritual, people, we should strive for self-preservation and also for compassion, particularism and also universalism.

CHAPTER 16

Protesting God
Rebellious Prophets and Human Morality

JONAH DOES NOT ALWAYS uphold the values that a prophet needs to carry with him, but eventually he submits to divine authority. He is a rebel prophet, but he is also a servant of God. Like other prophets, he is bound by his sacred duties to profess God's word and call for others to repent for their wickedness, but Jonah's approach contrasts with that of his predecessors. Let's examine some of these earlier scenarios.

Abraham, in one of his finest moments, attempts to persuade God not to destroy the morally bankrupt cities of Sodom and Gomorrah. He pleads with God, arguing that collective punishment is not the answer:

> Abraham then came forward and said, "Will You indeed sweep away the innocent along with the wicked? Suppose there are fifty innocent in the city—will You indeed sweep away the place, and not spare it for the sake of the fifty innocent who are in its midst? Far be it from You to do such a thing, killing innocent and wicked alike, so that the innocent and the wicked suffer the same fate. . . . Must not the Judge of all the earth do justly? (Genesis 18:23–25)

Generations later, Moses must bring the enslaved Hebrews out of Egypt and to the Promised Land. God's wrath against the recalcitrant Egyptians even extends to anger toward the newly liberated Israelites. Moses argues with God not to destroy his people:

> But Moses implored the Eternal his God saying, "Let not Your anger, Eternal One, blaze forth against Your people, whom You delivered from the land of Egypt with great power and with a mighty hand." (Exodus 32:11)

Rashi comments:

> "Leave Me alone!" So far we have not heard that Moses had prayed
> on their behalf, and yet God says, "Leave Me alone!" [which implies
> a refusal to his entreaty]. By saying this, God showed Moses a pos-
> sibility. God taught Moses: "If you pray for them, I will not destroy
> them. This depends on you."[219]

There is an inherent dignity in being a creature of God. Abraham
and Moses recognize the value of a human life, and they go out of
their way to protect those whom others would callously dismiss as
the enemy devoid of dignity or value. Their activism makes them
spiritual role models.

Jonah is different. When he has the opportunity to save a wicked
people, he responds as follows:

> He went down to Jaffo and found a ship going to Tarshish. He paid
> the fare and went aboard to sail with the others to Tarshish, away
> from the service of the Eternal. (Jonah 1:3)

While Abraham and Moses do all they can to save others, Jonah flees
from his duty. Still, Abraham and Moses do not submit blindly to
divine command. Just like Jonah, they also feel empowered to challenge God's judgment. Abraham and Moses are reluctant to submit
to God, because they are attempting to save lives. Jonah runs from
such a responsibility. None of the three believe that everything that
God says is right.

The prophet Jeremiah also challenges God's justice:

> You will win, O Eternal, if I make claim against You, yet I shall
> present charges against You: Why does the way of the wicked pros-
> per? Why are the workers of treachery at ease? You have planted
> them, and they have taken root, they spread, they even bear
> fruit. You are present in their mouths, but far from their thoughts.
> (Jeremiah 12:1–2)

Remarkably, God does not respond with rage when challenged by
prophets. Presumably, this is because such minor acts of rebellion
are seen as an exercise in moral reasoning, strengthening religious
impulse and deepening moral intuition.

King David asks the same question of God:

> Why have You hidden Your face? You have forgotten our affliction, our oppression—For our being is bowed down to the dust, our belly binds itself to the earth. Arise, be a help for us, and redeem us for the sake of Your covenantal love. (Psalm 44:25–27)

And so does another prophet, Habakkuk:

> How long, O Eternal, shall I cry out and You not listen, shall I shout to You, "Violence!" and You not save? Why do You make me see iniquity, [why] do You look upon wrong?—Raiding and violence are before me, strife continues and contention goes on. (Habakkuk 1:2–3)

To be a prophet seems to almost require a willingness to stand up and speak truth to power, even divine power.

A different reaction to the evil in our world is displayed in the Book of Job, where Job addresses God with the following words:

> By God who has deprived me of justice! By Shaddai who has embittered my life! As long as there is life in me, and God's breath is in my nostrils, my lips will speak no wrong, nor my tongue utter deceit. (Job 27:2–4)

Part of the maturation of the spirit is managing complexity. The evil in our world might numb us, but it might also awaken us to rise and fight for kindness and justice; lack of justice might infuriate us, but it might also deepen our relationship to God and our understanding of our own responsivity. Many biblical texts seem out of step with our contemporary understanding of equality, dignity, and human rights. Yet, these same texts also help us to develop kindness and generosity, as well as to protect the vulnerable. It takes the proper mindset to study problematic texts, which in turn allows us to sharpen our moral forthrightness and intellectual vigor.

On Morally Difficult Texts

We are all familiar with the tactics of extremists who distort religious beliefs to advance their own personal hatred. Fortunately, most people in our society recognize and reject these tactics. But how would we respond to a skeptic who points to a morally troubling verse, such as "And the Eternal your God delivers them to you and you defeat them, you must doom them to destruction: grant them no terms and give them no quarter" (Deuteronomy 7:2)? How do we reconcile the many admonitions in the Bible to be kind to strangers with a verse such as: "In the towns of the latter peoples, however, which the Eternal your God is giving you as a heritage, you shall not let a soul remain alive" (Deuteronomy 20:16) and with "Samuel said to Saul, 'I am the one the Eternal sent to anoint you king over God's people Israel. Therefore, listen to the Eternal's command! . . . Now go, attack Amalek . . . Spare no one, but kill alike men and women, infants and sucklings, oxen and sheep, camels and asses!'" (1 Samuel 15:1–3)? If taken too literally, these verses suggest that genocide is part of Jewish practice, which has never been true. Rather, we understand that these words are meant to be illustrative rather than actionable.

There are four primary philosophical approaches in relating to difficult texts within the faith tradition:

1. The "divine command morality" argument: Because God is the Source of and determines all morality, there is no contradiction between morality and God's commands. Only the Divine can understand the big moral picture, and thus only God has moral reasoning and authority. However, this argument asks us to abandon some of our God-given gifts, such as moral conscience, reason, and autonomy.

2. The argument proposed by Søren Kierkegaard (1813–1855): If there appears a contradiction between religion and morality, it is only because God has the power to suspend morality, and we must abandon our human conscience in heroic sacrifice to the divine command. The problem here is that we must consciously act against

our own moral intuition, which is spiritually and socially dangerous.

3. The "heretical argument": When faced with a contradiction between morality and religious command, we must choose morality. People acting on the basis of the "heretical argument" may be moral, but they are generally not deemed religious.

4. The "casuistic argument": Through moral reasoning, we come to understand and embrace the divine command. When we rely on both human morality and divine command, all contradictions can be resolved. We are never compelled to conform to anything immoral if we cultivate our intellectual and spiritual faculties to understand that religion and morality can always be reconciled.

This fourth approach is most compelling—and demanding—for the contemporary struggling to find meaning in their faith. Saadyah Gaon (ca. 880s–942, modern-day Iraq) explains that if we find a contradiction between tradition and reason, then we have made a mistake and must continue to study and analyze the text until text and reason are consistent. The text is only a starting place, to be read charitably and with a critical eye. At no time, however, should we neglect the human faculty of moral reasoning.

Rabbi Abraham Isaac HaKohen Kook writes:

> It is forbidden for religious behavior to compromise a personal, natural, moral sensibility. If it does, our fear of heaven is no longer pure. An indication of its purity is that our nature and moral sense becomes more exalted as a consequence of religious inspiration. But if these opposites occur, then the moral character of the individual or group is dismissed by religious observance, and we have certainly been mistaken in our faith.[220]

Although Jonah is the central figure of this book, we should not emulate him. Rather, we might emulate Abraham, who challenged a divine decree when he thought it was misguided. We should challenge dogmas to find the truth, remembering that the best reason for studying our sacred texts is not to puzzle over troublesome passages or to justify the behavior of another era, but to become motivated to act, today, in the true spirit of repairing our broken world.

CHAPTER 17

When God Renounces
A Theology of Change

> *And God renounced the punishment God had planned to bring upon them, and did not carry it out.*
> —Jonah 3:10

A BRAIN TEASER: If God created the vastness of the universe and found it perfect, then why would God create within the Divine Self any doubt? Does God have the capacity to doubt, to have second thoughts, to learn, to change God's opinion? If God learns, regrets, and repents with us, then we can share a real relationship. If God suffers along with the victims of injustice, then our experiences of divine immanence and alienation from the Divine are intertwined. If humans are created "in the image of God" (*b'tzelem Elohim*), then human redemption is interconnected with divine reality. Godliness is here on earth, inherent to our lives.

Jonah 3:10 seems clear, but the brevity of the verse hides its complexity. Is God changing and growing with us? Does God evolve, adapt with the times, and experience redemption? Is this an authentic Jewish theology? What does this mean for Jonah? And what does this mean for us?

According to Rashi's interpretation of Deuteronomy 30:3,[221] the Torah states that a living God is able to repent. A dynamic and evolving Divine Presence (*Sh'chinah*) goes into exile, returning when we restore the Divine Presence to the lower world and heal our relationship with God. According to Jewish tradition, God in fact changes positions, feels regret, learns from humanity, and destroys previous worlds that do not live up to their potential.

These teachings need not be read literally, but instead can be interpreted spiritually. Rabbi Bachya Ibn Pakuda (1050–1120, Spain), a mystic of the Neoplatonic variety, argued that the duties of the heart are on a separate plane from rational physical reality.[222] Certain truths can only be understood on an emotional and spiritual level. One is to "know God" with the heart.

God's repentance is not a response to some divine sin—this would not correspond with traditional understandings of God. Rather, God's repentance shows God in search of an evolved completeness, a wholeness that expands from the limited to the infinite. God is *absolutely* free. Free will is the means to all repentance. In the process of repenting, divine energy reinvigorates the world by the emanation of divine blessing, and divine self-revelation emerges in every moment and being. In this repentance, the divine essence remains constant, but God's relationship to Creation evolves as certain divine dimensions are affected by human action and moved in the direction of total unity.

Rabbi Kook explains that the Divine can be experienced as a kaleidoscope of constantly shifting colors.[223] God is intimately connected with humankind and responds to our brokenness and scattered spiritual state. The Deity is dynamic; divine manifestations are continually changing and renewing themselves. Reality is not so much an immutable physical substance as it is an evolving experience.

The Chasidic concept of *dirah batachtonin* (Aramaic for "living in the lower reaches") says that God dwells in the earthly realm, enabling connection between the physical and spiritual dimensions of reality.[224] God contains the universe but is more than the universe. If the world evolves, then God evolves, because God is in relationship with a progressing universe and is affected by humans. To state that God is not capable of expanding, growing, and adapting would be to limit divine omnipotence. Perfection is not static or stale; perfection is a state of constant growth, in which possibility continues to reach a higher actualization.

One test for theological truth asks whether the soul is transformed when the truth is embraced. Another test is whether the soul speaks to global injustice. Judaism teaches that *tikkun olam*—literally "repairing the world"[225]—involves a divine-human partnership. In a world where billions of people live in poverty, orphans are put into slavery, and widows are raped, one can relate only to a God who cries and suffers alongside us. The divine brokenness accompanies the journey of human brokenness, and together we heal.

If the capacity to repent represents the pinnacle of the human condition, then certainly repentance is a process in which we are to emulate God—a concept known as *halachta bidrachav* ("walk in God's path"; Deuteronomy 28:9). This concept of imitation must include self-improvement or risk inconclusiveness. God is an ideal for us only if we can actually emulate the divine ways. This image of God as One who grows, cries, and seeks liberation and unification is moving, especially in moments of deep vulnerability.

Rabbi Kook teaches that we are responsible for expanding, beautifying, and celebrating God's presence in this world. One way this is achieved is by seeking human healing and ensuring progress toward a just and holy world. The divine promise of growth for everything in the universe—including Godself—serves as our reminder and motivation that a better future is always attainable.

CHAPTER 18

Human Wrath
*On Climate Change and Weapons
of Mass Destruction*

NOWHERE IN THE BOOK OF JONAH does the narrative specifically describe the crimes of Nineveh. The rabbis, however, suggest that the crimes primarily involved robbery and violence. The immorality of Nineveh's people reminds the reader of the people among whom Noah lived. Once, when the world was full of chaos and moral disarray, God proposed mass destruction. Yet, after the Flood, God decreed that such an act will never be repeated: "Never again will I bring doom upon the world because of what people do" (Genesis 8:21). With Nineveh, God must now keep that promise, even if Jonah refuses to abide by it.

Jonah finds himself in an uncomfortable position. He needs to warn the Ninevites but does not know what to warn them of. He does not want to warn the Ninevites at all, because they are Israel's enemy. Should they repent and be saved, he might look like a false prophet and endanger the future of his own people. Should they not believe him, they might laugh at him or even endanger his own life. Whichever decision he makes, he cannot be certain that it will be to his favor—or to the favor of the people he loves. He is called to operate solely on the basis of his moral consciousness—and his love for God.

Abarbanel teaches that the message of Jonah's prophetic mission is unclear.[226] God never says that Nineveh would be destroyed if the Ninevites do not repent. God merely says that in forty days the city will be "overturned" (*neh'pachet*; Jonah 3:4), which might mean "transformed" rather than "destroyed." A mere human, Jonah is unable to comprehend God's plan to redeem the Ninevites. Erica Brown writes about Jonah's possible misunderstanding:

Jonah is *only* told to give a warning. But God does not indicate any actual plan of destruction, and He certainly does not tell Jonah to build an Ark. Ironically enough, when Jonah eventually gives his warning, it is not a warning at all—it is a declaration of doom that suggests a flood. . . . By stubbornly re-interpreting God's command—to merely warn Nineveh—into a veritable flood prophecy resembling that of Noah, Jonah expresses his clear dissatisfaction with God's recent dry spell and makes clear his wish for a reintroduction of floods into the world.[227]

Scholars argue that Jonah was afraid to be deemed a *navi sheker*—a "false prophet." The integrity of his name and his entire legacy was at stake.[228] But Abraham Ibn Ezra disagrees that Jonah feared this false title, for three reasons. First, Jonah was not initially told the full extent of the consequences of his potential failure; only in verse 4:2 does Jonah learn that Nineveh could have been destroyed if its people did not repent. Additionally, Jonah would not have feared being called a false prophet if the prophecy itself were real. And finally, the people of Nineveh would come to understand that because they had repented, they had averted destruction. Ibn Ezra argues that Jonah resisted acting on the prophecy because he felt it unfair that Nineveh, Israel's enemy, be given the chance to repent.[229]

Perhaps Jonah hesitates to voice his prophecy because he fears being thought a liar or overly dramatic, pessimistic, and antagonistic. The rabbis say:

> [Jonah] was sent to Jerusalem to prophesy destruction; when [the Jerusalemites] repented, God had mercy . . . and did not destroy it, and they called him a false prophet. The third time [Jonah was called], he was sent to Nineveh to cry its destruction. Jonah thought to himself: "I know that the gentiles are near repentance and they will indeed repent. . . . Not only will Israel call me a false prophet, but even pagan worshipers will call me a false prophet. I will flee to a place where God's glory is not present.[230]

The Ishbitzer Rebbe, a nineteenth-century Chasidic rabbi known for his work *Mei Hashilo'ach*, suggests that perhaps Jonah was also afraid he would not survive the destruction of the city: "The prophet feared being in the city because he was sure that at least a few houses or courtyards would fall."[231]

A prophet has access to a special truth that most do not, but only God has access to perfect truth. Jonah only has his own sense of what is good and right—and still, he needs to make decisions.

Today, when facing current ecological and political questions, we seem to be in a similar situation.

National security and special governmental intelligence units, as well as scientists researching environmental destruction, have access to the most advanced data and tools, but their calculations can never be completely perfect. We know the threats posed by white supremacy, terrorism, and unchecked patriarchy, but we are afraid to get involved. The challenge is both social and epistemological: not only do we fear the reactions of others to our convictions and actions, but we can also never be sure that our convictions are entirely true. And still, we have to act, because even though God's covenant with humanity is that God will not destroy the world, we have no promise that humanity will not destroy itself.

Two of the greatest threats to humanity are climate change and nuclear weapons.

Climate Change

Climate change, and its potential to destroy the delicate balance of nature, is one of the world's most immediate challenges. The scientific consensus is that we humans must change our ways or risk extinction. Unfortunately, demagogues have exploited the issue, citing God's promise to Noah that the world will not be destroyed (Genesis 8:21). While God will surely uphold God's promises, we have to face the fact that humanity's myopia, greed, and constant need to plunder endanger the earth and our existence on it.

One of the tragic effects of climate change is the extinction of animal species.[232] A majority of scientists believe that the earth is now experiencing the sixth mass extinction event in its history, with extinctions occurring at nearly ten thousand times the normal expected rate. While previous extinctions were largely caused by space debris or geological disruption, today's mass extinction is the work of human beings.

Animal habitats are being destroyed at unprecedented rates. As the earth's surface warms, millions of species will simply disappear.

The consequences of climate change are dire:

- About a third of about sixty-three hundred species of amphibians face extinction due to their sensitivity to climate change, a rate that is twenty-five thousand to more than forty-five thousand times greater than what would normally be expected.
- It is estimated that about half of all mammal species—including humans, gorillas, monkeys, lemurs, and animals beyond primates—are at risk of extinction from loss of habitat and climate change.
- A World Wildlife Fund report, as analyzed by the Zoological Society of London, of more than fifty-eight hundred fish populations in the world's oceans concluded that the number of fish in the world's oceans has declined by nearly 50 percent since 1970, due to overfishing as well as rising ocean water temperatures caused by global climate change. In North America, the American Fisheries Society estimates that seven hundred species of fish are in danger of extinction, representing nearly 40 percent of all fish.
- Trees are not exempt from climate change and weather extremes. During the current four-year drought in California, about twelve million trees have died. Incredibly, even the massive sequoia trees, some of which have lived thousands of years, are showing unprecedented stress, including the shedding of leaves much earlier than usual.

While climate change is a perilous challenge to overcome, nature is resilient. So is the human spirit to effect positive change. We dare not retreat in the face of challenges. Rather, we must prepare for them (personally and collectively) and adapt to new realities. Sometimes we must look beyond our fears and misgivings to redeem the world.

Nuclear Weapons

Recent world events remind us of the threat of nuclear weapons. On the one hand, most officials and ordinary citizens decry the unprecedented destructive capacity of nuclear warheads, yet nearly every nation wants to possess them, on the grounds of deterrence or intimidation. Only the future can reveal how dangerous this paradox is.

In 1945, newly inaugurated as commander-in-chief after the death of Franklin D. Roosevelt, Harry S. Truman became the first figure to deploy a nuclear weapon against another population. On August 6, 1945, the United States dropped the first atom bomb in human history. The blast burned with a heat equal to that of the sun, instantly vaporizing and incinerating thousands of people in Hiroshima. It completely destroyed a two-mile impact area, annihilated two-thirds of all buildings within a three-mile radius, and killed nearly three hundred thousand people.

On August 9, 1945, the Americans dropped a second bomb near the city of Nagasaki. Though much less destructive than the bombing of Hiroshima, this bombing inflicted tens of thousands of deaths and injuries. While many Americans credit the bombings with ending the war, scholars suggest that the declaration of war by the Soviet Union presented a much more immediate threat to the Japanese.

The Cold War era revealed that its nuclear arsenal would not provide the level of security the United States had hoped for. The Soviet Union developed its own atomic bomb in 1949, prompting the United States to develop the exponentially more powerful hydrogen bomb in 1952. The Soviet Union responded with the production of their own H-bomb the following year.

When President Dwight D. Eisenhower came into office in 1953, he faced the difficulty of maintaining American military strength while not "wasting money" on unnecessary military spending. Eisenhower decided to cut the army budget while greatly increasing spending on nuclear weapons, long-range bombers, submarines, and intercontinental ballistic missiles (ICBMs). His first secretary of defense, Charles E. Wilson, called it "a bigger bang for the buck." The Eisenhower administration believed that nuclear weapons would suppress any Soviet invasion of Europe ("massive retaliation") and eventually destroy the Soviet Union.

Eisenhower's Soviet counterpart, Nikita Khrushchev, emerged as first secretary in 1956. Khrushchev, keenly aware that the Soviet Union lagged behind the United States technologically and militarily, resorted to a bluff. He went so far as to claim at the United Nations in 1960 that the Soviets produced ICBMs like "sausages" on an assembly line. Only in the ensuing decades have we come to learn that the United States dominated the decade in nuclear weapon production and test explosions.

President John F. Kennedy came into office as a hawk, having campaigned against a mythical "missile gap" with the Soviets. Khrushchev responded in 1961 with the largest nuclear test explosion in history, a fifty-megaton blast that frightened the American public. It was the ultimate bluff: the bomb weighed sixty thousand pounds and could not have been delivered as a weapon. In reality, the Soviets had about six ICBMs capable of reaching the United States, versus hundreds of American warheads that could reach the Soviet Union. Later, in a move to counter American missiles in Turkey, Khrushchev agreed to install ICBMs in Cuba (after an aborted CIA-sponsored invasion). The resulting crisis nearly plunged the world into nuclear war. Fortunately, it led to the Nuclear Test Ban Treaty (1963), which banned aboveground nuclear testing, greatly reducing the amount of radiation released into the atmosphere.

Khrushchev's successor, Mikhail Gorbachev, made dramatic changes upon coming to power in 1985. One move was a unilateral moratorium on nuclear tests from August 1985 to February 1987. In 1986, the United States conducted fourteen tests, and that same year Gorbachev proposed eliminating all nuclear warheads by the year 2000; President Reagan initially agreed to an immediate elimination. Reagan's advisers immediately persuaded him to drop the idea, unwilling to give up its space-based nuclear defensive system development program. In December 1987, the United States and the USSR signed a treaty to eliminate intermediate-range nuclear forces (INF). Throughout the INF Treaty, the USSR eliminated fifteen hundred missiles, and the United States destroyed about half that number.

Today's most distressing hot spot for nuclear activity is in the rogue state of North Korea. In 1945, Kim Il-sung emerged as the nation's autocratic leader and, in 1950, launched an invasion of South Korea in an effort to unify the nation under his control. The brutal war that followed, in which the newly established United Nations voted to aid the South, ended in stalemate in 1953, although no peace treaty was ever signed. In the succeeding years, Kim at times seemed to endorse unification and nuclear nonproliferation, even joining the United Nations in 1991. When Kim died in 1994, his son Kim Jong-il took over and signed an agreement freezing North Korea's nuclear weapons program in exchange for fuel and two light-water nuclear reactors. In the ensuing years, moments of hope for a peaceful unification were countered by hostile declarations, economic decline, and even famine. In 2006, North Korea detonated its first nuclear bomb, and the United Nations responded with economic sanctions.

Kim Jong-un, who succeeded his father in 2011, has continued pushing the envelope of international limits on nuclear weapons. The mysterious leader has generally increased the pace of nuclear development, and though there are attempts at détente, North Korea continues to be a worrisome hot spot for weapons development.

The threat of nuclear warfare continues to loom, despite there being no political objective worth the horrific death of countless people. We would do well to heed the voice of one witness from Hiroshima: "I touched and smelled Hell." We must understand just how great is the danger, with the wrong people in power, of the world being blown to pieces at the slightest whim. Former secretary of state Colin Powell commented, "I . . . declare my hope and declare it from the bottom of my heart that we will eventually see the time when that number of nuclear weapons is down to zero and the world is a much better place."

Jonah's desire to see the destruction of a people rather than seeking their redemption parallels recent history's folly for destruction and domination. Like Jonah, contemporary humanity, too, prefers destruction over working for its own redemption—or the redemption of others. However, while Jonah wants to punish, God wants to redeem!

For the untold generations that will hopefully grow up in a world without the constant threat of destruction at a moment's notice, Jonah's story should be a clarion call to always strive to see the spark of holiness in everyone and everything, to correct the mistakes of the past, and to always seek a brighter future—even if we might lose face, have to work hard, and may never be entirely certain that we will succeed.

CHAPTER 19

Jonah and Job
Responsibility, Comfort, and Joy

Prophetic Responsibility

Is Jonah an effective leader, a great congregator of souls, a conveyor of passionate truths, a spokesman for a generation? One reading of the biblical text suggests that Jonah is unfit for leadership: he shirks his obligations as a prophet, flees at the first sign of trouble, and offers no reason to command the Ninevites' respect. The genius of Jonah's designation as a prophet in the canon, however, is that despite his outer flaws, he demonstrates inner strength.

The Book of Job and the Book of Jonah complement one another, as both figures go through enormous hardship. Both speak to God's desire to test the mettle of humanity. Both ask if people can cope with enormous challenges. However, Job, a simple and holy man, asks theological questions, while Jonah is mostly silent, keeping concerns to himself. Job asks why God takes lives and objects belonging to Job himself, why he should suffer, why his faith is being tested thus, and how he can remain a humble servant of God while the world crumbles around him. Jonah, on the other hand, experiences inner conflict rather than a physical threat to his security. His struggles with God manifest through doubt and rumination. Jonah seeks escape at sea, refuge on a ship, and isolation in a fish, unaware that what he most needed protection from was his own crisis of faith.

Can we trust a prophet whose primary move is to run when confronted by the slightest risk? It is anathema to Jewish tradition to venerate someone so self-interested. Jonah behaves antithetically to what is expected of an emissary of God.

James Kugel offers a counter-narrative to explain Jonah's peculiar mind-set. Kugel asserts that Jonah is not running from responsibility but is protective of the noble status of the prophet:

> The most basic thing about prophecy is that God is supposed to let the prophet's words "fall to the ground" (I Samuel 3:19); in other words, everything a true prophet says must come to pass. Indeed, the very definition of a false prophet is one who announces something "but the thing does not take place or prove true" (Deuteronomy 18:22). Jonah therefore feels betrayed.[233]

A sense of betrayal inspires irrationality, such as fleeing from one's God-given duties. Being unprepared to face one's duties is a mark not of weakness, but of modesty and humility. Jonah needs to introspect before he can overcome obstacles.

Rashi explains that when Jonah is in the belly of the great fish, he can peer out of the fish's eyes. Though seemingly anatomically impossible, this action is rich in metaphor. The fish's eyes are windows that peer only into the imperceptible depths of the unexplored sea.[234] Thus, when Jonah looks out of the eyes of his captor, he peers into infinite blackness, vast oceans of potential. The belly of the fish is the sanctuary where Jonah discovers his true self. Like the traditional design of the synagogue, in which the sanctuary has at least one window to allow people to peer outside, the fish allows Jonah to pray, think, and exalt to the heavens—while not secluding himself, instead looking out at the greater world to intertwine his inner and outer lives.

Dr. Martin Luther King Jr. peered into darkness and saw potential, too. A modern prophet, he worked to transform his inner fears into sources of vision and joy. On the night before his assassination in April 1968, Dr. King said:

> Well, I do not know what will happen now. We've got some difficult days ahead. But it does not matter with me now. Because I've been to the mountaintop. . . . And I've looked over. And I've seen the promised land. . . . I'm not fearing any man.[235]

To be a moral leader, one must lead a contemplative life of spiritual reflection, embrace darkness, and reject cynicism in favor of positivity. The cost of these ideals can be high, but the benefits are immense. And, for the organized soul, the benefits are eternal.

Must a Prophet Be Rich?

Torah commentators furiously debate the necessity of a prophet's wealth. The Talmud teaches that Jonah paid for everyone's fare on the ship because he was in a rush to escape.[236] Based on that Talmudic explanation, Rabbi David Kimchi says that the profession of prophecy falls upon those who are privileged with inexhaustible means.[237] Rabbi Nissim of Gerona, known as the Ran (1320–1376, Spain) argues that a prophet must be wealthy so that people respect them.[238] Centuries later, Maimonides, influenced by the Aristotelian notion that wealth is closely linked with virtue, writes that the verse actually refers to *spiritual* wealth, not *financial* wealth.[239]

Wealth, however, does not permit hedonism. Those who view financial means as a qualification to be a prophet presumably believe that someone with monetary wealth has more resources than others to learn and to cultivate virtue.[240] Abarbanel argues that wealth is the outcome, not the course, of cultivating prophetic virtues.[241] Those of independent financial means[242] have sufficient power and privilege to speak out against the most powerful people without jeopardizing their own security.[243] People like that should use their position to "speak truth to power."[244] On the other hand, Maimonides believed that prophets should possess no wealth other than the word of God to guide them. In fact, several prophets—namely Isaiah, Jeremiah, and Ezekiel—issued scathing critiques of the rich for their thievery and oppression of others. However, if the prophets were wealthy, they were not criticized for their wealth.

In our time, we see little to no correlation between wealth and prophetic leadership. But the rabbis proposed that a prophet required wealth in the biblical era.[245] It seems that a prophet should have something to lose. A prophet who is poor is possibly more able to take a risk because there is nothing to lose. A prophet of means, however, could choose a life of luxury and exclusion but instead chooses the path of God. With this, the prophet becomes a model for each of us.

A Joyful Calling

Whether or not a prophet should have financial wealth, we do know that a prophet must have inner joy:

> Rabbi Yochanan said: "Jonah ben Amitai was among the holiday pilgrims. He entered the water libation festival, and the holy spirit rested upon him. This teaches us that the holy spirit rests only on one who is happy of heart."[246]

From these lessons, we glean that we must invest in spiritual wealth if we are to succeed in life. Monetary wealth is important for survival, but obsession with maintaining wealth damages our potential to repair our broken world.

Prophets are not perfect, nor are they always the most forthright in their deeds; Jonah behaves like a broken man. His journey is one of repeated failure on the brink of success, reminding us that no one is perfect. Each of us has flaws to work on improving, just as our society always needs improvement.

Finally, Jonah teaches us that having the strength to recognize our weaknesses and channeling those deficits into strength will get us far in life.

Jonah's sojourn within the fish is a fantastical manifestation of these ideas, but one that we can also apply to our own routines. Encasing ourselves in a healing space that separates us from the vituperation of the world is a healthy way to reorient our priorities. While we should be deeply concerned about the state of affairs in society, we should also cultivate our personal relationships to the Divine. Only then will we be able to maintain inner joy.

CHAPTER 20
Gilgulim
The Jewish Theology of Reincarnation

WHY DO THE PEOPLE of Nineveh have forty days to repent? Rabbi Zvi Grumet lists some parallels with this specific number:

> In both biblical and rabbinic stories the number forty represents birth and rebirth. In the Bible, Moses is on the mountain for forty days and emerges as a man reborn with a radiant face. The spies enter the land as princes and forty days later return with the self-image of grasshoppers. The Israelite nation spends forty years in the desert and is transformed from a fractured nation of refugees into a unified nation of conquerors. . . . In rabbinic literature, there are forty minus one categories of prohibited (creative) work on Shabbat, a child is considered to be "alive" in the womb after forty days, and pregnancy lasts for forty weeks.[247]

Going beyond the abstract notion of rebirth, Rabbi Yisrael Meir Kagan, the halachist and writer known as the Chofetz Chayim (1839–1933, Russia and Poland), suggests that in the Book of Jonah is a hidden message about reincarnation: none of us can perfect ourselves in this life, which is why we need multiple attempts.[248] Such a reading is supported by Elijah ben Solomon Zalman, the Vilna Gaon (1720–1797, Lithuania):

> The extent to which this theme is interwoven into the fabric of *Sefer Yonah* is truly noteworthy. In addition to the factual, true account of Yonah's mission, the Vilna Gaon (throughout his commentary to *Sefer Yonah*) perceives an allegorical interpretation within the text. Yonah is the *n'shamah*, which is charged with a mission to fulfill in this world: perfecting the soul. The *n'shamah* boards a "vessel" to journey through this world: namely, the body. But the person tries to flee from *Hashem* and avoid fulfilling His charge. Eventually, the individual is "swallowed up" and departs from this world,

leaving his task unfinished. What happens after that? "And the Word of *Hashem* came to Yonah a second time, saying: 'Arise! Go to Nineveh . . .'" (Jonah 3:1–2). The *n'shamah* is sent back to earth, to finally accomplish its intended mission. [249]

Reincarnation occurs when the human soul returns to earth in a new body after death. Many cultures have their own opinions on how and if this mechanism occurs. Even within individual cultures, divergent views abound. For example, Jewish medieval theologians took various approaches in arguing for the existence of *gilgulim* ("reincarnation"). For these learned scholars, reincarnation can be viewed as a response to the problems of theodicy[250] or as an opportunity for spiritual and intellectual improvement.

Rabbi Yitzchak Saggi Nahor, also known as Isaac the Blind (HaBahir, 1160–1235, France), argues in *Sefer Habahir* that transmigration, the re-embodiment of souls, offers a compelling response to the question of theodicy. How can it be that righteous people suffer? He answers that a righteous individual suffers as the result of wrongs done in a previous existence. The soul of this righteous person is in fact not entirely as virtuous as it appears.

One century later in Spain, Nachmanides and Rabbeinu Bachya both argue fiercely for transmigration and hold that certain *mitzvot* can only be understood with reference to the concept of *gilgulim*. The classic example is *yibum* ("levirate marriage"), a ritual that brings a deceased person's soul back into the world through the marriage of a widow to her husband's brother.

The Kabbalist Rabbi Chayim Vital (1542–1620, Safed and Damascus) argues in his magnum opus *Sha'ar Hagilgulim* that transmigration is important because it gives humans the potential to seek growth, perfection, and actualization. He writes that one must fulfill the *taryag mitzvot* ("the 613 commandments of the Torah") in order to achieve complete *d'veikut* ("intimacy with the Infinite") and that we must learn the Torah in all four of the traditionally conceived approaches (namely *p'shat*, *remez*, *d'rash*, and *sod*: "the simple read, the hinted, the Midrashic, and the mysterious"). We return to a new life in order to attempt to master our comprehension of *torat chayim* ("the living Torah").

Those three primary arguments for *gilgulim* are a response to the problems of theodicy, a way to explain certain *mitzvot*, and an opportunity for spiritual and intellectual actualization.

Reincarnation can be seen as a progressive theology that allows us to combat racism, sexism, speciesism, and many of society's other ills. There is a Kabbalistic idea that a righteous person who sinned returns to this world after death as a soul transmigrated into a fish.[251] While a theology promoting "heaven" offers an escape from the iniquities of this world, reincarnation theology delves further into the goodness of life. It reinforces that we are eternally earthly creatures. Our souls are not complete until we reach a level of worldly achievement. The soul needs a new body in which to continue striving before it can achieve a final state of completion.

How do we reconcile this with the concept of *olam haba* ("the World-to-Come, the afterlife") and the importance we place on reaching it?

Whether or not we believe that reincarnation adequately addresses certain issues of theodicy or earthly justice, the concept of reincarnation raises new and exciting theological possibilities. It offers the chance for improved morality—to be better parents, more ethical consumers, more spiritually minded in our endeavors, or more philanthropic in our nature. A theology of the *interconnectedness* of all souls offers great potential for our moral lives, suggesting a spiritual paradigm for universal love and solidarity. When we encounter another living being, we see how our existences are intertwined. Through the realization that we may have had shared experiences in a past life or perhaps will have shared experiences in a future life, we cultivate greater compassion for those who are different from ourselves. From this mind-set, reincarnation is a moral concept that is concerned with taking responsibility for our past, present, and future. Such a theology of reincarnation does not make life less important than afterlife, but rather makes us responsible for the moral quality of our lives, our complete existence, all of Creation, and eternity.

In the Jewish concept of reincarnation, the return to this world is not a punishment, but rather a vote of confidence that we can ultimately succeed in the schemes of life. While there is no proof of what happens to the soul after death, our theology about any sort of afterlife should guide us to become better people. If we love all life, we must seek and crave its eternal perpetuation. We are asked to take responsibility for our full existence, even the existence that we cannot touch or see.

Even if we hold our theologies with some skepticism and not the fervent certainty of fundamentalists, we might ask how our relationships with other creatures make us more complex people. The Book of Jonah reminds us that animals are not only sentient beings, but in some way are a part of society. They may even have some role in bringing about redemption, just as the fish helped Jonah realize that God, Creation, and nature are limitless. The Book of Jonah thus allows us to seek the beauty in animals, the perpetuation of the soul through nature, and their connection with the Divine.

CHAPTER 21

The Element of Change
Water as a Theological Metaphor

WATER IS HUMBLE. It has a basic molecular structure and yet the power to grant life and death. Water covers over 70 percent of the earth's surface and makes up almost the same percent of our bodily composition.[252] Water sustains all life. We must work collectively to avoid flooding, droughts, and water pollution—deadly plagues for much of humanity.[253] Today, our contact with fresh water sources and crop irrigation is much less direct than in the past, so it is all the more important to cultivate an appreciation for the water that keeps us alive.[254]

The prophet Amos refers to water as a bringer of justice (Amos 5:24) and a metaphor for Torah. Additionally, many biblical verses consider water a significant means of purification.[255] Consider the High Holy Day ritual of *tashlich*, during which people symbolically throw bread into the water as a means to atone for sins.[256] Water can be used in ritual life to elevate our consciousness. We can immerse ourselves in a *mikveh*, and we can wash our hands upon waking in the morning and before eating bread with the traditional blessing of *n'tilat yadayim*, to remind us how dependent we are—as is all life— on water. Because of Miriam's merit, the Talmud teaches, a well traveled with the Israelites throughout their journeys in the desert.[257] Later, the Israelites sang to God in gratitude for the water they had (Numbers 21:17). "They traveled three days in the wilderness and found no water" (Exodus 15:22), but when they did, it was a cause for celebration. The prophet Jeremiah referred to God as the "Source of living waters," understanding that water is the sustainer of all life (Jeremiah 2:13, 17:13). In ancient Jewish theology, rain is connected with divine blessing. This is reflected in the *Sh'ma* prayer (see Deuteronomy 11:14) that is traditionally read twice daily. The prophet Isaiah states that "joyfully shall you draw water from the foundations of triumph" (Isaiah 12:3). This connection is made because water symbolizes resurrection and rebirth (Isaiah 26:19). In the Book of Job (Job 38:8), primordial waters are compared to a watery womb, from which birth occurs. In the Book of Psalms, God creates waters but splits their power into both chaotic hurricanes and calm peaceful streams (Psalm 104). The dual nature of water is that it can both heal and hurt. The ability to swim can be necessary for survival. For this reason, there is a rabbinic imperative specifically to teach our children to swim[258] and more generally to respect water and use it wisely.

For Jonah, water is an omen of ill will, obstruction, even death (Jonah 2). The Book of Jonah reminds us to be conscious of the way water influences human interaction with the world and each other. The sea carries us from one continent to the next, it nourishes our bodies and souls, and it fosters life. But water is also unyielding and unforgiving. It crushes and swallows people whole. Life in the water terrifies as much as it intrigues. Jonah finds revelation in the water and its creatures. He finds clarity in its opaque depths, breathes in life at water's most unhospitable spot, and emerges from the water as a changed man.

Water is purity, wrath, and peace. It is cruel, redemptive, and destructive. Water is the culmination of every aspect of life on this planet.[259] For Jonah, land represents a monotonous, firm way of life, while water represents chaotic disorder, but also boundless potential. This can be true for us as well.

We cannot expect a giant fish to save us from the chaotic waves of landless existence, but that does not mean we can abandon hope for a renewed world. Each action we take toward creating a more verdant earth affords us the opportunity to bring back an existence more harmonious with nature.

CHAPTER 22

Jonah's Tomb
On Jewish-Muslim Relations in a Pluralistic World

JONAH IS AN IMPORTANT PROPHET not only in Judaism, but also for our Abrahamic cousins, Christianity and Islam. The story of Jonah (or *Yunus*) is addressed in the tenth chapter (*surah*) of the *Qur'an*, where he is considered an obedient and honorable prophet.[260] Jonah is referred to as *Dhul-Nun* ("The One of the Fish"), serving as a reminder that Jonah is only granted life after his residency within the great leviathan because he submitted to the will of God.[261]

I will be the first to point out that my specialty is Judaism, not Islam, but I have been fortunate enough to make friends with and learn from many leaders and allies in the Muslim community. One of the most powerful lessons I have learned is that Islam, like Judaism, uses the Jonah narrative to instill the importance of being nonjudgmental. The Prophet Muhammad teaches, "One should not say that I am better than Jonah."[262] In a *midrash* from *Pirkei D'Rabbi Eliezer*, Jonah could see out of the eyes of the fish, while the ninth-century Islamic Persian historian Al-Tabari writes that the fish was transparent, enabling Jonah to see the "wonders of the deep."[263] The two religious traditions seem to have similar interpretations of this perplexing story.

The mosque and shrine atop Nabi Yunus in Mosul was dedicated to the prophet Jonah and served as a symbol of unity for all Abrahamic faiths. In 2014, during a disturbing wave of violence, the terrorist group known as the Islamic State of Iraq and Syria (ISIS) destroyed Christian sites, including the traditional site of Jonah's final resting place. These fanatics deemed shrines idolatrous in the view of the Muslim faith.[264]

One interpretation of this violence says that Jonah felt the people of Assyria irredeemable, and the destruction of his tomb may have confirmed his view that the people of Nineveh would return to wickedness. We must take care not to let our anger over ISIS's actions lead to Islamophobia. People of all faiths—including other Muslims—have suffered greatly from these monstrous activities, and mainstream Islam claims Jonah as a prophet whose legacy should be honored rather than desecrated. Perhaps ISIS's outrageous destruction deepens the relationship between Jews and Muslims, as does the Book of Jonah itself, and moves us toward compassion.

Islam in Jewish Thought

Though Jewish thought does not view Islam as idolatry, commentators have been careful to distinguish the differences between the faith traditions. Maimonides, who lived and worked among Muslim elite,[265] writes:

> These Muslims . . . are not in any way idolaters. [Idolatry] has already been removed from their mouths and their hearts, and they unify God in the appropriate manner. . . .[266]
> All the words . . . of this Ishmaelite [i.e., Muhammad] . . . are only to make straight the path for the messianic king and to prepare the whole world to serve the Lord together. As it is said: "For then I will make the peoples pure of speech so that they all invoke the Eternal and serve God with one accord" (Zephaniah 3:9).[267]

The Muslim people are our cousins and today—in America, in Israel, and in other countries where Jews can meaningfully participate in public discourse—we should combat rampant Islamophobia, advocate for Muslim protection, and foster solidarity with their communities. Rabbi David Rosen, of the American Jewish Committee and a bridge builder par excellence, in 2012 stated:

> On the basis of the position of the Meiri (*Bet Habehirah* on the Babylonian Talmud, *Bava Kama* 113b) recognizing both Muslims and Christians as monotheistic believers bound by the minimal moral code, the first Ashkenazi Chief Rabbi in Israel, Rabbi Avraham Yitzchak HaCohen Kuk ruled (*Iggeret* 89; *Mishpat-Cohen* 63) that Muslims and Christians living in a predominant Jewish society must be treated . . . with full civil liberties, just like Jews.[268]

Anxiety and resentments about geopolitical events, undergirded by long-standing mutual suspicion, keep Jewish and Muslim communities wary of each other. This is a lamentable by-product of fundamentalist-wrought pain. As humble figures looking to build and heal the rifts between our communities, we should partner now to foster understanding, harmony, and better relations. No matter the difficulty, we *must* create opportunities for the Jewish and Muslim communities to become allies.

We live in an age in which discontent and uncertainty have turned their wrathful eyes toward minority communities. The international turmoil over the past few years can easily cast doubt on the hope for bridge building. The refugee crisis in Europe, the frustrating resurgence of antisemitism and rise of Islamophobia, and the radical polarization of political ideologies can leave us feeling hopeless. But respect, mutual understanding, and empathetic connection are still possible. One of our most critical tasks is to create opportunities for young Jews and Muslims to regularly engage in dialogue. We can do this through the most ancient of traditions: communicating and sharing meals. In both Jewish and Muslim traditions, Abraham models this practice. In the Hebrew Bible and the *Qur'an*, Abraham opened his home to three strangers who turned out to be emissaries of God (Genesis 18), teaching us the value of radical compassion for strangers. Rather than attending one-and-done events or participating in surface-level interfaith gatherings, true dialogue between Jews and Muslims sparks an exciting renaissance for those who seek substantive meaning. We are not so naïve as to imagine that dialogue without action is the way to solve all problems and tensions between faith communities. However, we have to start somewhere.

Men with hate in their hearts may have physically destroyed Jonah's tomb, hoping to put a wedge between great nations. But their sledgehammers do not break our will. They did not destroy the need for mutual respect, even in times where division seems the easiest route to follow. We must rise to rebuke the hateful violence of terrorist groups. We must stand united for peace and justice. Jonah's memory is a uniting force for us all.

Jewish and Muslim communities are no strangers to global discord and tension and are divided further with the rise of radical demagogues. Those committed to pluralism and inclusion know that the Jewish and Muslim communities must come together to serve as role models for religious freedom. Today, as essential freedoms are being challenged, we must safeguard these liberties for all people, not just ourselves. The diversity in democracies around the world is worth defending and preserving for future generations. With the most modest of actions, there is hope not only for a renewal in relations between great religious traditions, but also for a more enlightened discourse for our communities all over the world.

CHAPTER 23

Between Joy and Exhaustion
The Jonah Complex and the Human Condition

ABRAHAM MASLOW (1908–1970), one of the twentieth century's preeminent thinkers on the human condition, devised the psychological condition known as the "Jonah complex." The limitation of one's self-actualization puzzled Maslow, and he sought to determine the symptoms and remedies to such perplexing behaviors. Maslow writes:

> We all have unused potentialities. . . . It is certainly true that many of us evade our . . . suggested vocations. . . . So often we run away from the responsibilities dictated (or rather suggested) by nature, by fate . . . just as Jonah tried—in vain—to run away from *his* fate.[269]

Maslow believed that many people sabotage their own potential. For Maslow, Jonah perfectly exemplifies these neuroses: a prophet who cannot, for unknown reasons, fulfill his mission with the same acuity of his prophetic forbears.

Maslow argues that just as Jonah ran from his destiny, so are many of us afraid of fulfilling our life's purpose. Perhaps we fear making a life commitment to an intimate partner, making major career transitions, moving to other locations, pursuing art or thrills, or, simply, enjoying domesticity. We all fear something and we all carry self-doubt. Are we afraid of failure, accepting responsibility, letting down our loved ones, the guilt that accompanies success, a change in our lifestyle, or others' judgment?

Social justice workers are familiar with the overwhelming feeling that the work will never be complete. This despair often leads to moral paralysis, which avoids action entirely. Using Jewish ideals to change the world for the better can be intimidating, as there is so much work to be done. If we never complete the larger goals, however, we will never be whole. Until the day that we pass from the earth, we will be unable to fully step back and throw in the towel. Rabbi Judah Loew ben Bezalel, known as the Maharal (1520–1609, Prague), teaches about the individual's need to push forward even when it is difficult:

> A human is not created in their final wholeness. Humans were created to actualize their wholeness. That is the meaning of the verse "Humans were born to toil." Humans are born and exist for the aim of this toil, which is the actualization of our potential. One can, however, never attain the state of actualized being. One must toil forever, to actualize one's wholeness. . . . Even when one attains a certain level of actualization, one still remains potential, and will forever have to go on actualizing oneself.[270]

How can we apply these notions to our lives today? The quest for perfection is, in many respects, limiting and hazardous. And while each of us has unique potential to become who we are meant to be during our short days on earth, each of us also has our own barriers to living out this mission.

We are "born to toil"; giving up is not an option. We must constantly strive to become whole even if we never truly succeed. This human need for a sense of completion and wholeness is only achieved through partnership; wholeness is found in the uniting of disparate souls.

The late theologian and Emory University professor James Fowler (1940–2015) describes the highest stage of human spiritual development as follows:

> Fascinated with the charisma, the authority and frequently the ruthlessness of [certain] leaders, we must not fail to attend to . . . the criteria of inclusiveness of community, of radical commitment to justice and love and of selfless passion for a transformed world, a world made over not in their images, but in accordance with an intentionality both divine and transcendent.[271]

We have the capacity improve the world while striving for spiritual fulfillment and further attachment to justice. The Talmud teaches that "one only learns Torah in areas where one's heart has desire."[272] Too often, we choose tasks that numb us rather than rouse us to our most excited state.

Awaken!

Awaken today!

Awaken every day!

There is no time to wander or escape. We must pursue the work that our souls crave. We must build our spiritual activist communities so that they are inclusive of individuals' diverse ways of doing good.

Now, this spiritual hedonism is justified when it produces the desire to express pure happiness and positivity. This is the underlying value of Rabbi Joseph Soloveitchik's argument:

> Compassion is the socialized expression of joy. A person is summoned to serve God by serving his fellow man when he is least inclined to place himself at the disposal of others, when he is preoccupied with himself and the only service to which he attributes any value is self-service. He is contented with himself; he has been successful, he rejoices at his own great achievements, and he is ready to shut out the world in his exaltation over his marvelous self. Exactly then, the call to service sounds.[273]

There is virtue that can come from egocentrism, self-indulgence, and perhaps even arrogance. When spiritual fulfillment and self-actualization are sought and elevated to the most pressing moral tasks, our holy work can be done. Our primary focus should be supporting those marginalized, but we must also embrace self-actualization in order to do justice.

What was the cause of Jonah's personal complex? Did he fear being unable to live up to his last name, *ben Amitai*, "a person of truth"? Did he fear being unable to fulfill the meaning of his first name, *yonah*, the "dove," which symbolizes his identity as a messenger of peace? Was he afraid that his legacy would be that of false prophet? Was he overwhelmed by his own insignificance in the vastness of the universe or by the greatness of his mission? Maslow agrees that Jonah could have feared such heavy responsibility,[274] loss of control, or even death.[275] If Abraham is the prophet who journeys forth fearlessly to a foreign land at great risk, then Jonah serves as the foil who runs away from the foreign land to which he is called.

There will always be people destined to outshine us. We cannot let the achievements of others make us lose pride in our own achievements. We keep climbing and use the deeds of others to inspire us and help pull us up.

Perhaps we should coin a new term: the "Nineveh complex." If the Jonah complex means one who bars one's own success, then perhaps a Nineveh complex is one who too readily assumes success. If there is humility to Jonah's uncertainty of himself, then perhaps there is arrogance in the residents of Nineveh. While we are to be optimistic, we must also be realistic and, more importantly, humble. Each day, we are called to take another small step closer to Nineveh and away from Tarshish. When we falter, we need not punish ourselves, but rather recognize, "Ah, there is my Jonah complex. I'm not a failure. I'm not going backward. I'm just living my Jonah complex right now." We can then realign ourselves with our higher purpose. Jonah was given more than one chance to fulfill his tasks. We, too, may fail and try again. We may fear that someone will knock us over or that we will collapse. However, we hold a sense of "trust" (*bitachon*) that we can survive the "spiritual journey" (*avodah*). Though difficult, it is ultimately rewarding.

CHAPTER 24: THE IMPERFECT JEWISH HERO | 121

CHAPTER 24
The Imperfect Jewish Hero
Encountering Moral Ambiguity with Compassion

THE IDEA THAT every biblical character personifies perfection is commonplace. After all, the Jewish tradition (and much of Western civilization's tradition) is built on the foundation that the words of the Bible are unerring in their direction toward a life of holiness and piety.[276] There are still readers who feel uncomfortable with the idea of analyzing or critiquing a biblical character as someone who is less than perfect. Such a narrative runs counter to the one presented during elementary religious education, as well as popular examinations of biblical figures. It is rather apparent in the text, however, that the actions (and reactions) of many biblical figures are imperfect, because the Bible is not meant to display the perfection of the human being, but rather humanity's divinely inspired limitations.

The need to sing the praises of our biblical figures may in many ways be counterproductive to our development. When we blindly accept every biblical figure as morally perfect, we deny ourselves the right to read the biblical texts critically and the obligation to tackle moral ambiguity and arrive at differentiated and complex answers. Can we rationalize all of Jonah's activities as ethically forthright? A simple answer would obviously be in the negative: Jonah behaves in ways that do not comport with the normative actions of a prophet. But by reconsidering his story from multiple perspectives and with compassion, we are able to see Jonah as a hero of sorts: Jonah's charge to Nineveh gains much in spiritual clarity, but at a significant price to Jonah's psyche and, perhaps, even his being.

In a moving passage, Rabbi Aharon Lichtenstein (1933–2015) writes that the need to exalt biblical figures is a backward way of looking at the tradition. As spiritual beings ourselves, we are not meant to look at the Bible in a sterile manner, but to read between the lines. As Rabbi Lichtenstein postulates:

> Advocates of hagiographic *parshanut*, which portrays the central heroic figures of scriptural history as virtually devoid of emotion, can only regard the sharpening of psychological awareness with reference to Tanakh with a jaundiced eye. But for those of us who have been steeped in *midrashim*, [Nachmanides], and [Naftali Zvi Yehuda Berlin also known as Ha'amek Davar]—in a tradition, that is, which regards the patriarchal *avot* and their successors as very great people indeed but as people nonetheless, and which moreover sees their greatness as related to the their humanity— enhanced literary sensibility can be viewed as a significant boon.[277]

Facing multifaceted moral texts, we cannot engage in mere polemics. We honor biblical figures by treating them as humans and not as agents with supra-human abilities.[278] King David, whose lineage is said to bring about the redemption of the world, sinned enormously during his lifetime. But his flaws did not keep him from being one of Israel's greatest leaders, whose literary contributions shaped countless hearts and whose wisdom modeled deep introspection and repentance. Still, no one can point to David and say truthfully that he was an unequivocal paragon of ethics.[279] It is vital to learn from morally complex leaders because the human condition is riddled with ethical paradox. Studying the stories of such figures found throughout the Torah only adds layers of intellectual nuance and spiritual discovery.

Consider this fascinating *midrash* that relates to all humanity as "broken vessels":

> Rabbi Alexandri said: If a commoner uses a broken vessel, it is a disgrace to them. But the Holy One of Blessing uses broken vessels, as it says: "God is close to the brokenhearted" (Psalm 34:19); [and as it says:] "Who heals the brokenhearted" (Psalm 147:3).[280]

It is not only the great achievements, extraordinary actions, and inner deeds of the Bible's figures that make them worthy of study.

The greatest takeaway from the Bible is how these figures handled their public challenges and personal struggles. There is a beautiful and limitless spirituality that can be cultivated with this approach to imperfection.

The late Leonard Cohen, a musician whose sagacity was manifest in the poetry of his lyrics, sings, "There is a crack in everything / That is how the light gets in."[281] Jonah gifts us with a unique portrayal of the humanity of a prophet. We may feel uncomfortable critiquing Jonah simply because of his status as a prophet. However, we should feel a bit uncomfortable analyzing or judging any person, prophet or not, who deviates from the image of a perfect soul.

Our task is to not be satisfied with the simple answers or straightforward understandings of good and evil. Instead, we strive toward the shades of gray and moral subtlety. We redeem our souls through deeper understanding of Creation's greatest mysteries.

CHAPTER 25

Caring about the City
A Theology of Compassion

> *You cared about the plant, which you did not work for and which*
> *you did not grow, which appeared overnight and perished over-*
> *night. And should not I care about Nineveh, that great city, in*
> *which there are more than a hundred and twenty thousand per-*
> *sons who do not yet know their right hand from their left, and*
> *many beasts as well!*
> —Jonah 4:10–11

AS OUR TRAVELS AND TRAVAILS with Jonah come to a close, we still
do not know Jonah's fate. Does Jonah repent and completely submit
to God's will? Does he run away again? Does he move to Nineveh?
Does he kill himself in despair? Is he righteous or a reprobate in a
prophet's robes? Is he full of fear or full of hatred? Is he humble or
arrogant? We simply do not know.

But perhaps we do not need to know. Perhaps it is not on us to
arrive at a final judgment of Jonah and his deeds. What we learn is
that Jonah is like us—complex.

Because the Book of Jonah does not end on a high note, tradition
adds the last three verses of the prophecy of Micah when it is read on
the afternoon of Yom Kippur.[282]

The final questions of the story remain unanswered, proving the
power of the absence of words. This absence prompts us to imagine
the scenarios that descend upon Jonah at the conclusion of his journey. Rabbi Chaim Jachter writes:

> There is only one [other] instance in Tanach where a narrative ends
> with a question. . . . Genesis chapter 34 ends with Shimon and
> Levi's response to [Jacob's] criticism of their violent reaction to the

kidnapping of Dinah. Shimon and Levi ask, "Shall we tolerate our sister being treated as a harlot?" [Jacob's] response to this question is not recorded.[283]

One *midrash* understands Jonah's silence at the end of the book as a token of submission:

> Immediately Jonah fell upon his face and stated, "God, I recognize that I sinned before You. Forgive me for fleeing to the sea, as I was unaware of Your great might, which I now recognize."[284]

Mother Teresa said: "Silence of the heart is necessary so you can hear God everywhere—in the closing of a door, in the person who needs you, in the birds that sing, in the flowers, in the animals."[285] Maybe Jonah keeps silent in order to make space for God and God's view of his story. What did God say to Jonah before this story? What did God say to Jonah after this story? Is this book the full extent of their relationship? We just do not know. We might write a fifth chapter entertaining the possibilities: does Jonah die, repent, return to Israel, or move to Nineveh? The rabbis suggest, as a possible fifth chapter, that Jonah finally came around and prayed that God be merciful.[286] Abarbanel teaches that Jonah lost his prophetic status because he was not obedient enough.[287]

Ending the book with a question is a powerful rhetorical device. Does the author believe the reader cannot handle the conclusion? Perhaps the author themself cannot handle it. Are we to allow our moral imagination to draft the conclusion? Perhaps, if this story is really about us and our lives, each of us has a different conclusion that we must choose and reaffirm.

No one comforts Jonah; he is lonely and depressed. Sometimes those most hardened by the world and lacking social comfort have the most trouble with feeling compassion. Thus, an action as simple as a hug can be transformative. Consider the view of Matthew Sanford, a nationally recognized master of yoga and interpersonal connectivity, on the need to break out of one's aloofness to bring comfort at critical moments:

There's a reason why, when my son who's six is crying, he needs a hug. It's not just that he needs my love. He needs a boundary around his experience. He needs to know that the pain is contained and can be housed and it will not be limiting his whole being. He gets a hug and he drops into his body.[288]

Change is difficult, but the compassion of others makes it easier.

Joseph Campbell, the late professor of mythology and comparative religion, writes, "We must be willing to let go of the life we've planned, so as to have the life that is waiting for us."[289] To do so, we must embrace loss *and* the support of others as we accept the challenges of moving forward. Leaders cannot become isolated prophets. Only through collaborative work, "hugging" each other, can we weather the storms.

Rabbi David Kimchi asks why in Hebrew Scriptures there is a book entirely about a gentile nation (Nineveh) without any mention of Israel.[290] He answers that it is a moral lesson for Israel: If other nations can repent before God, then we can repent as well.

The Book of Jonah urges us to foster interpersonal relationships over those with the material world. Adam and Eve find their downfall from a tree. Similarly, Jonah slides to his final downfall from a plant. Both in Genesis and in Jonah, the characters' desires for material comfort[291] overcome their charge to fulfill a holy mandate. Jonah struggles with his mandate. God says to him, "You cared about the plant, which you did not work for and which you did not grow, which appeared overnight and perished overnight. And should not I care about Nineveh, that great city, in which there are more than a hundred and twenty thousand persons who do not yet know their right hand from their left, and many beasts as well!" (Jonah 4:10–11). If Jonah feels such pity toward the plant,[292] then how much more should God pity the people of Nineveh? Yet, even with his misplaced priorities, Jonah is remarkably successful. Jonah's speech—merely five words (Jonah 3:4)—brings about Nineveh's repentance. What makes Jonah's prophecy so effective? Without textual evidence, some commentators suggest that Jonah might not have been alone after all.[293] Because Jonah was unknown and without status in Nineveh, people would not have listened to him. He must, therefore, have had a partner. Jonah did embark with company; he embarked on his journey with the sailors, who represent all the nations of the world.[294] Those sailors, more than anything else, are teachers of compassion: they have mercy on Jonah, a stranger to them, and do everything they can to save him from God's hand.

Susan Sontag (1933–2004) explains the consequences of not acting upon compassion:

> Compassion is an unstable emotion. It needs to be translated into action, or it withers.[295] The question is what to do with the feelings that have been aroused, the knowledge that has been communicated. People do not become inured to what they are shown. . . . It is passivity that dulls feeling.[296]

The Book of Jonah urges us to stay focused and to not let our hearts get hardened: We must remain open, compassionate, and receptive of miracles. Rabbi Lawrence Kushner writes:

> Look more closely at the process of combustion. How long would you have to watch wood burn before you could know whether or not it actually was being consumed? Even dry kindling wood is not burned up for several minutes. This then would mean that Moses would have had to watch the "amazing Sight" closely for several minutes before he could possibly know there even was a miracle to watch! . . . The "burning bush" was not a miracle. It was a test. God wanted to find out whether or not Moses could pay attention to something for more than a few minutes. When Moses did, God spoke. The trick is to pay attention to what is going on around you long enough to behold the miracle without falling asleep. There is another world, right here within this one, whenever we pay attention.[297]

Conclusion

OUR MOST IMPORTANT takeaways from Jonah are these profound messages:

- God cares for all people. God's infinite wisdom is beyond that of humans. We cannot fathom the layers of reality that exist for God, but we *can* understand that all humans were created in God's image, and thus God works for the well-being of all people. God cares for those who do good, as well as for those who sin.

- God's mercy outweighs God's justice. God does not want to destroy the world just because one person strays from God's divine plans. If that were the case, the earth would be cinders due to the deeds that we do every day. God understands that humanity is far from perfect and wants us to learn from our mistakes in order to become better because of them. Each day is another opportunity to become the person we are born to be.

- We resemble Jonah, fleeing responsibility and returning to it. Jonah is emblematic of the flawed spiritual seeker. He behaves in a cowardly fashion, though his mission is to be resolute in his truth. Jonah is no closer to God than you or I. Jonah is us, and we are Jonah.

- One cannot flee from God. None of us can escape our destiny no matter how hard we struggle against it. Our souls are bound together through a shared lineage of holiness. This irrevocable bond with others and with the Divine is both our burden and our challenge. We should not run from it, but leap toward it. We may stumble and fall, but we can keep getting back up until our purpose in this universe is actualized.

- It is too reductive to judge Jonah with sweeping gener-
  alizations. Like most of us, he is complex and evolving,
  lonely and lost. He appears to be lacking family, friends,
  community, and a clear sense of purpose. In the end, he
  may appear transformed, but we cannot know that for
  sure. He becomes a mirror to our own existential angst, to
  our own wandering souls and to the issues of transformation that we must now face.

Members of the Jewish community—from the youngest toddlers
to the heads of influential institutions, to those simply trying to find
their place within the larger fabric of the Jewish world—know the
challenge of balancing obligation to the community with the need to
grow as spiritual beings. We all do the best we can to shoulder our
diverse spiritual, communal, and personal responsibilities. However, Jewish life is so crowded with noise that it is easy to become
trapped within the minutiae and miss the universal ethical messages.
Jonah reorients us all to examine our deficits in order to turn them
into strengths. We do not have to be the most learned or admired
person to discover our talents, as they reside within us, oftentimes
just below the surface.

Sometimes our failures are crucial parts of our journey. The mys-
tics suggest that God, who has a hand in everything, even helped
Jonah to flee.[298] The idea is that the ship had already departed two
days earlier, but God sent a wind to send the ship back to Jonah so
that he could board it to Tarshish. For us too, sometimes a setback is
just a crucial part of our life journey.

Though this exploration is nearly at a close, it is not truly the
end for us. There is always more holy truth to find in the prophet's
journey. Perhaps a deeper look will provide your own answers to
this book's most irregular profile of a prophet. For me, Jonah's
heart remains an enigma; yet, we can learn so much from it. Jonah's
shortcomings—as a prophet, a man of piety, and a friend—allow us
to peer inside the heart of someone whose virtue is that he does not

have all the answers, even with access to the word of the Divine. We lack this access but still walk away with the ability to make judgments based on ethical truths and moral realities, the greatest insights to God's desire for humankind.

Biblical scholar Judy Klitsner writes:

> The open question with which the Book of Jonah concludes suggests that while there is no guarantee that humanity will embrace the opportunities for self-transformation, it is indeed possible for them to produce constructively subversive sequels within their own lives.[299]

We all live with paradoxes and pitfalls. The human condition is complex. We have our own traumas and glories, our major failures and heroic moments. Our task is not simply to feel motivated by our highs, but also to not let our lows pull us down. We must live with the hope that today, or at least tomorrow, we can do better than we did today—for ourselves and for the world around us.

The following text of the Book of Jonah is from the
*JPS Hebrew-English Tanakh: The Traditional Hebrew
Text and the New JPS Translation* by permission of
the University of Nebraska Press. Second edition,
copyright © 1999 by The Jewish Publication Society,
Philadelphia.

The Book of Jonah
Hebrew and English

CHAPTER I

The word of the Lord came to Jonaha son of Amittai: 2 Go at once to Nineveh, that great city, and proclaim judgment upon it; for their wickedness has come before Me. 3 Jonah, however, started out to flee to Tarshish from the Lord's service. He went down to Joppa and found a ship going to Tarshish. He paid the fare and went aboard to sail with the others to Tarshish, away from the service of the Lord.

4 But the Lord cast a mighty wind upon the sea, and such a great tempest came upon the sea that the ship was in danger of breaking up. 5 In their fright, the sailors cried out, each to his own god; and they flung the ship's cargo overboard to make it lighter for them. Jonah, meanwhile, had gone down into the hold of the vessel where he lay down and fell asleep. 6 The captain went over to him and cried out, "How can you be sleeping so soundly! Up, call upon your god! Perhaps the god will be kind to us and we will not perish."

7 The men said to one another, "Let us cast lots and find out on whose account

1 וַיְהִי דְּבַר־יְהֹוָה אֶל־יוֹנָה בֶן־
אֲמִתַּי לֵאמֹר: 2 קוּם לֵךְ אֶל־
נִינְוֵה הָעִיר הַגְּדוֹלָה וּקְרָא עָלֶיהָ
כִּי־עָלְתָה רָעָתָם לְפָנָי: 3 וַיָּקׇם
יוֹנָה לִבְרֹחַ תַּרְשִׁישָׁה מִלִּפְנֵי
יְהֹוָה וַיֵּרֶד יָפוֹ וַיִּמְצָא אֳנִיָּה |
בָּאָה תַרְשִׁישׁ וַיִּתֵּן שְׂכָרָהּ וַיֵּרֶד
בָּהּ לָבוֹא עִמָּהֶם תַּרְשִׁישָׁה
מִלִּפְנֵי יְהֹוָה:

4 וַיהֹוָה הֵטִיל רֽוּחַ־גְּדוֹלָה
אֶל־הַיָּם וַיְהִי סַעַר־גָּדוֹל בַּיָּם
וְהָאֳנִיָּה חִשְּׁבָה לְהִשָּׁבֵר: 5 וַיִּירְאוּ
הַמַּלָּחִים וַיִּזְעֲקוּ אִישׁ אֶל־אֱלֹהָיו
וַיָּטִלוּ אֶת־הַכֵּלִים אֲשֶׁר בָּאֳנִיָּה
אֶל־הַיָּם לְהָקֵל מֵעֲלֵיהֶם וְיוֹנָה
יָרַד אֶל־יַרְכְּתֵי הַסְּפִינָה וַיִּשְׁכַּב
וַיֵּרָדַם: 6 וַיִּקְרַב אֵלָיו רַב הַחֹבֵל
וַיֹּאמֶר לוֹ מַה־לְּךָ נִרְדָּם קוּם
קְרָא אֶל־אֱלֹהֶיךָ אוּלַי יִתְעַשֵּׁת
הָאֱלֹהִים לָנוּ וְלֹא נֹאבֵד:

7 וַיֹּאמְרוּ אִישׁ אֶל־רֵעֵהוּ לְכוּ
וְנַפִּילָה גוֹרָלוֹת וְנֵדְעָה בְּשֶׁלְּמִי

this misfortunehas come upon us."
They cast lots and the lot fell on Jonah.
8 They said to him, "Tell us, you who
have brought this misfortune upon
us, what is your business? Where have
you come from? What is your country,
and of what people are you?" 9 "I am
a Hebrew," he replied. "I worship the
Lord, the God of Heaven, who made
both sea and land." 10 The men were
greatly terrified, and they asked him,
"What have you done?" And when the
men learned that he was fleeing from
the service of the Lord—for so he told
them—11 they said to him, "What must
we do to you to make the sea calm
around us?" For the sea was growing
more and more stormy. 12 He answered,
"Heave me overboard, and the sea will
calm down for you; for I know that
this terrible storm came upon you on
my account." 13 Nevertheless, the men
rowed hard to regain the shore, but they
could not, for the sea was growing more
and more stormy about them. 14 Then
they cried out to the Lord: "Oh, please,
Lord, do not let us perish on account
of this man's life. Do not hold us guilty
of killing an innocent person! For You,
O Lord, by Your will, have brought this
about." 15 And they heaved Jonah overboard, and the sea stopped raging.

16 The men feared the Lord greatly;

הָרָעָה הַזֹּאת לָנוּ וַיַּפִּלוּ גּוֹרָלוֹת
וַיִּפֹּל הַגּוֹרָל עַל־יוֹנָה: 8 וַיֹּאמְרוּ
אֵלָיו הַגִּידָה־נָּא לָנוּ בַּאֲשֶׁר לְמִי־
הָרָעָה הַזֹּאת לָנוּ מַה־מְּלַאכְתְּךָ
וּמֵאַיִן תָּבוֹא מָה אַרְצֶךָ וְאֵי־מִזֶּה
עַם אָתָּה: 9 וַיֹּאמֶר אֲלֵיהֶם עִבְרִי
אָנֹכִי וְאֶת־יהוה אֱלֹהֵי הַשָּׁמַיִם
אֲנִי יָרֵא אֲשֶׁר־עָשָׂה אֶת־הַיָּם
וְאֶת־הַיַּבָּשָׁה: 10 וַיִּירְאוּ הָאֲנָשִׁים
יִרְאָה גְדוֹלָה וַיֹּאמְרוּ אֵלָיו מַה־
זֹּאת עָשִׂיתָ כִּי־יָדְעוּ הָאֲנָשִׁים כִּי־
מִלִּפְנֵי יהוה הוּא בֹרֵחַ כִּי הִגִּיד
לָהֶם: 11 וַיֹּאמְרוּ אֵלָיו מַה־נַּעֲשֶׂה
לָּךְ וְיִשְׁתֹּק הַיָּם מֵעָלֵינוּ כִּי הַיָּם
הוֹלֵךְ וְסֹעֵר: 12 וַיֹּאמֶר אֲלֵיהֶם
שָׂאוּנִי וַהֲטִילֻנִי אֶל־הַיָּם וְיִשְׁתֹּק
הַיָּם מֵעֲלֵיכֶם כִּי יוֹדֵעַ אָנִי כִּי
בְשֶׁלִּי הַסַּעַר הַגָּדוֹל הַזֶּה עֲלֵיכֶם:
13 וַיַּחְתְּרוּ הָאֲנָשִׁים לְהָשִׁיב אֶל־
הַיַּבָּשָׁה וְלֹא יָכֹלוּ כִּי הַיָּם הוֹלֵךְ
וְסֹעֵר עֲלֵיהֶם: 14 וַיִּקְרְאוּ אֶל־
יהוה וַיֹּאמְרוּ אָנָּה יהוה אַל־נָא
נֹאבְדָה בְּנֶפֶשׁ הָאִישׁ הַזֶּה וְאַל־
תִּתֵּן עָלֵינוּ דָּם נָקִיא כִּי־אַתָּה
יהוה כַּאֲשֶׁר חָפַצְתָּ עָשִׂיתָ:
15 וַיִּשְׂאוּ אֶת־יוֹנָה וַיְטִלֻהוּ אֶל־
הַיָּם וַיַּעֲמֹד הַיָּם מִזַּעְפּוֹ:
16 וַיִּירְאוּ הָאֲנָשִׁים יִרְאָה

they offered a sacrifice to the Lord and
they made vows.

CHAPTER 2

The Lord provided a huge fish to
swallow Jonah; and Jonah remained
in the fish's belly three days and three
nights. 2 Jonah prayed to the Lord
his God from the belly of the fish.
3 He said:

In my trouble I called to the Lord,
And He answered me;
From the belly of Sheol I cried out,
And You heard my voice.

4 You cast me into the depths,
Into the heart of the sea,
The floods engulfed me;
All Your breakers and billows
Swept over me.

5 I thought I was driven away
Out of Your sight:
Would I ever gaze again
Upon Your holy Temple?

6 The waters closed in over me,
The deep engulfed me.
Weeds twined around my head.

7 I sank to the base of the mountains;
The bars of the earth closed upon me
forever.
Yet You brought my life up from
the pit,
O Lord my God!

גְדוֹלָה אֶת־יהוה וַיִּזְבְּחוּ־זֶבַח
לַיהוֹה וַיִּדְּרוּ נְדָרִים:

1 וַיְמַן יהוה דָּג גָּדוֹל לִבְלֹעַ
אֶת־יוֹנָה וַיְהִי יוֹנָה בִּמְעֵי הַדָּג
שְׁלֹשָׁה יָמִים וּשְׁלֹשָׁה לֵילוֹת:
2 וַיִּתְפַּלֵּל יוֹנָה אֶל־יהוה
אֱלֹהָיו מִמְּעֵי הַדָּגָה: 3 וַיֹּאמֶר
קָרָאתִי מִצָּרָה לִי אֶל־יהוה
וַיַּעֲנֵנִי
מִבֶּטֶן שְׁאוֹל שִׁוַּעְתִּי
שָׁמַעְתָּ קוֹלִי:
4 וַתַּשְׁלִיכֵנִי מְצוּלָה
בִּלְבַב יַמִּים
וְנָהָר יְסֹבְבֵנִי
כָּל־מִשְׁבָּרֶיךָ וְגַלֶּיךָ
עָלַי עָבָרוּ:
5 וַאֲנִי אָמַרְתִּי
נִגְרַשְׁתִּי מִנֶּגֶד עֵינֶיךָ
אַךְ אוֹסִיף לְהַבִּיט
אֶל־הֵיכַל קָדְשֶׁךָ:
6 אֲפָפוּנִי מַיִם עַד־נֶפֶשׁ
תְּהוֹם יְסֹבְבֵנִי
סוּף חָבוּשׁ לְרֹאשִׁי:
7 לְקִצְבֵי הָרִים יָרַדְתִּי
הָאָרֶץ בְּרִחֶיהָ בַעֲדִי לְעוֹלָם
וַתַּעַל מִשַּׁחַת חַיַּי
יהוה אֱלֹהָי:

8 When my life was ebbing away,
I called the Lord to mind;
And my prayer came before You,
Into Your holy Temple.

9 They who cling to empty folly
Forsake their own welfare,a

10 But I, with loud thanksgiving,
Will sacrifice to You;
What I have vowed I will perform.
Deliverance is the Lord's!

11 The Lord commanded the fish, and it
spewed Jonah out upon dry land.

CHAPTER 3

The word of the Lord came to Jonah a
second time: 2 "Go at once to Nineveh,
that great city, and proclaim to it what
I tell you." 3 Jonah went at once to
Nineveh in accordance with the Lord's
command.

Nineveh was an enormously large
city—a three days' walk across. 4 Jonah
started out and made his way into the
city the distance of one day's walk, and
proclaimed: "Forty days more, and
Nineveh shall be overthrown!"

5 The people of Nineveh believed God.
They proclaimed a fast, and great and
small alike put on sackcloth. 6 When the
news reached the king of Nineveh, he
rose from his throne, took off his robe,

8 בְּהִתְעַטֵּף עָלַי נַפְשִׁי
אֶת־יְהוָה זָכָרְתִּי
וַתָּבוֹא אֵלֶיךָ תְּפִלָּתִי
אֶל־הֵיכַל קָדְשֶׁךָ:
9 מְשַׁמְּרִים הַבְלֵי־שָׁוְא
חַסְדָּם יַעֲזֹבוּ:
10 וַאֲנִי בְּקוֹל תּוֹדָה
אֶזְבְּחָה־לָּךְ
אֲשֶׁר נָדַרְתִּי אֲשַׁלֵּמָה
יְשׁוּעָתָה לַיהוָה:
11 וַיֹּאמֶר יהוה לַדָּג וַיָּקֵא אֶת־
יוֹנָה אֶל־הַיַּבָּשָׁה:

1 וַיְהִי דְבַר־יהוה אֶל־יוֹנָה
שֵׁנִית לֵאמֹר: 2 קוּם לֵךְ אֶל־
נִינְוֵה הָעִיר הַגְּדוֹלָה וּקְרָא
אֵלֶיהָ אֶת־הַקְּרִיאָה אֲשֶׁר אָנֹכִי
דֹּבֵר אֵלֶיךָ: 3 וַיָּקָם יוֹנָה וַיֵּלֶךְ
אֶל־נִינְוֵה כִּדְבַר יהוה
וְנִינְוֵה הָיְתָה עִיר־גְּדוֹלָה
לֵאלֹהִים מַהֲלַךְ שְׁלֹשֶׁת יָמִים:
4 וַיָּחֶל יוֹנָה לָבוֹא בָעִיר מַהֲלַךְ
יוֹם אֶחָד וַיִּקְרָא וַיֹּאמַר עוֹד
אַרְבָּעִים יוֹם וְנִינְוֵה נֶהְפָּכֶת:
5 וַיַּאֲמִינוּ אַנְשֵׁי נִינְוֵה
בֵּאלֹהִים וַיִּקְרְאוּ־צוֹם וַיִּלְבְּשׁוּ
שַׂקִּים מִגְּדוֹלָם וְעַד־קְטַנָּם:
6 וַיִּגַּע הַדָּבָר אֶל־מֶלֶךְ נִינְוֵה
וַיָּקָם מִכִּסְאוֹ וַיַּעֲבֵר אַדַּרְתּוֹ

put on sackcloth, and sat in ashes. 7And he had the word cried through Nineveh: "By decree of the king and his nobles: No man or beast—of flock or herd—shall taste anything! They shall not graze, and they shall not drink water! 8 They shall be covered with sackcloth—man and beast—and shall cry mightily to God. Let everyone turn back from his evil ways and from the injustice of which he is guilty. 9Who knows but that God may turn and relent? He may turn back from His wrath, so that we do not perish."

10God saw what they did, how they were turning back from their evil ways. And God renounced the punishment He had planned to bring upon them, and did not carry it out.

CHAPTER 4

This displeased Jonah greatly, and he was grieved. 2 He prayed to the Lord, saying, "O Lord! Isn't this just what I said when I was still in my own country? That is why I fled beforehand to Tarshish. For I know that You are a compassionate and gracious God, slow to anger, abounding in kindness, renouncing punishment. 3 Please, Lord, take my life, for I would rather die than live." 4 The Lord replied,

מֵעָלָיו וַיְכַס שַׂק וַיֵּשֶׁב עַל־הָאֵפֶר: 7 וַיַּזְעֵק וַיֹּאמֶר בְּנִינְוֵה מִטַּעַם הַמֶּלֶךְ וּגְדֹלָיו לֵאמֹר הָאָדָם וְהַבְּהֵמָה הַבָּקָר וְהַצֹּאן אַל־יִטְעֲמוּ מְאוּמָה אַל־יִרְעוּ וּמַיִם אַל־יִשְׁתּוּ: 8 וְיִתְכַּסּוּ שַׂקִּים הָאָדָם וְהַבְּהֵמָה וְיִקְרְאוּ אֶל־אֱלֹהִים בְּחָזְקָה וְיָשֻׁבוּ אִישׁ מִדַּרְכּוֹ הָרָעָה וּמִן־הֶחָמָס אֲשֶׁר בְּכַפֵּיהֶם: 9 מִי־יוֹדֵעַ יָשׁוּב וְנִחַם הָאֱלֹהִים וְשָׁב מֵחֲרוֹן אַפּוֹ וְלֹא נֹאבֵד: 10 וַיַּרְא הָאֱלֹהִים אֶת־מַעֲשֵׂיהֶם כִּי־שָׁבוּ מִדַּרְכָּם הָרָעָה וַיִּנָּחֶם הָאֱלֹהִים עַל־הָרָעָה אֲשֶׁר־דִּבֶּר לַעֲשׂוֹת־לָהֶם וְלֹא עָשָׂה:

1 וַיֵּרַע אֶל־יוֹנָה רָעָה גְדוֹלָה וַיִּחַר לוֹ: 2 וַיִּתְפַּלֵּל אֶל־יהוה וַיֹּאמַר אָנָּה יהוה הֲלוֹא־זֶה דְבָרִי עַד־הֱיוֹתִי עַל־אַדְמָתִי עַל־כֵּן קִדַּמְתִּי לִבְרֹחַ תַּרְשִׁישָׁה כִּי יָדַעְתִּי כִּי אַתָּה אֵל־חַנּוּן וְרַחוּם אֶרֶךְ אַפַּיִם וְרַב־חֶסֶד וְנִחָם עַל־הָרָעָה: 3 וְעַתָּה יהוה קַח־נָא אֶת־נַפְשִׁי מִמֶּנִּי כִּי טוֹב מוֹתִי מֵחַיָּי: 4 וַיֹּאמֶר יהוה

"Are you that deeply grieved?"

5 Now Jonah had left the city and
found a place east of the city. He
made a booth there and sat under it
in the shade, until he should see what
happened to the city. 6 The Lord God
provided a ricinus plant, which grew
up over Jonah, to provide shade for his
head and save him from discomfort.
Jonah was very happy about the plant.
7 But the next day at dawn God provided
a worm, which attacked the plant so
that it withered. 8 And when the sun
rose, God provided a sultry east wind;
the sun beat down on Jonah's head, and
he became faint. He begged for death,
saying, "I would rather die than live."
9 Then God said to Jonah, "Are you so
deeply grieved about the plant?" "Yes,"
he replied, "so deeply that I want to
die."

10 Then the Lord said: "You cared
about the plant, which you did not
work for and which you did not
grow, which appeared overnight and perished
overnight. 11 And should not I care about
Nineveh, that great city, in which there
are more than a hundred and twenty
thousand persons who do not yet know
their right hand from their left, and
many beasts as well!"

הֵיטֵב חָרָה לָךְ:
5 וַיֵּצֵא יוֹנָה מִן־הָעִיר וַיֵּשֶׁב
מִקֶּדֶם לָעִיר וַיַּעַשׂ לוֹ שָׁם סֻכָּה
וַיֵּשֶׁב תַּחְתֶּיהָ בַּצֵּל עַד אֲשֶׁר
יִרְאֶה מַה־יִּהְיֶה בָּעִיר: 6 וַיְמַן
יְהוָה־אֱלֹהִים קִיקָיוֹן | וַיַּעַל
מֵעַל לְיוֹנָה לִהְיוֹת צֵל עַל־רֹא
שׁוֹ לְהַצִּיל לוֹ מֵרָעָתוֹ וַיִּשְׂמַח
יוֹנָה עַל־הַקִּיקָיוֹן שִׂמְחָה
גְדוֹלָה: 7 וַיְמַן הָאֱלֹהִים
תּוֹלַעַת בַּעֲלוֹת הַשַּׁחַר
לַמָּחֳרָת וַתַּךְ אֶת־הַקִּיקָיוֹן
וַיִּיבָשׁ: 8 וַיְהִי | כִּזְרֹחַ הַשֶּׁמֶשׁ
וַיְמַן אֱלֹהִים רוּחַ קָדִים
חֲרִישִׁית וַתַּךְ הַשֶּׁמֶשׁ עַל־רֹאשׁ
יוֹנָה וַיִּתְעַלָּף וַיִּשְׁאַל אֶת־נַפְשׁוֹ
לָמוּת וַיֹּאמֶר טוֹב מוֹתִי מֵחַיָּי:
9 וַיֹּאמֶר אֱלֹהִים אֶל־יוֹנָה
הֵיטֵב חָרָה־לְךָ עַל־הַקִּיקָיוֹן
וַיֹּאמֶר הֵיטֵב חָרָה־לִי עַד־מָוֶת:
10 וַיֹּאמֶר יְהוָה אַתָּה חַסְתָּ
עַל־הַקִּיקָיוֹן אֲשֶׁר לֹא־עָמַלְתָּ
בּוֹ וְלֹא גִדַּלְתּוֹ שֶׁבִּן־לַיְלָה
הָיָה וּבִן־לַיְלָה אָבָד: 11 וַאֲנִי
לֹא אָחוּס עַל־נִינְוֵה הָעִיר
הַגְּדוֹלָה אֲשֶׁר יֶשׁ־בָּהּ הַרְבֵּה
מִשְׁתֵּים־עֶשְׂרֵה רִבּוֹ אָדָם אֲשֶׁר
לֹא־יָדַע בֵּין־יְמִינוֹ לִשְׂמֹאלוֹ
וּבְהֵמָה רַבָּה:

Notes

INTRODUCTION

1   Sennacherib (705–681 BCE), the head of the Assyrian Empire at the time, later waged war in the region, and particularly on Judea and the inhabitants of Jerusalem.

2   Scholars suggest that the book was probably actually written in the late fifth or early fourth century BCE. Fragments of the book were found among the Dead Sea Scrolls in the Qumran Caves.

3   Abraham Ibn Ezra on Jonah 3:3.

4   *B'reishit Rabbah* 98:11; *Pirkei D'Rabbi Eliezer* 33.

5   "Therefore, he was called Ben Amitai, as it says [about Elijah], 'The word of God on your lips is true [*emet*]' (I Kings 17:24)." Also see *Zohar* 2, Exodus 197a.

6   Mark Kleiman, "The Sullen Prophet: A Commentary on the Book of Jonah," *Atlantic*, August 10, 2010, https://www.theatlantic.com/entertainment/archive/2010/08/the-sullen-prophet-a-commentary-on-the-book-of-jonah/61210/.

7   For other prophets' reluctance, see, for instance, Moses in Exodus 3 at the Burning Bush, Jeremiah 1:6, and Isaiah 6:5. For more on this trend, see Sheldon H. Blank, *Understanding the Prophets* (New York: Union of American Hebrew Congregations, 1969), 35, 38–40.

8   *Babylonian Talmud, Sanhedrin* 89a.

9   Abarbanel on Jonah 1:12. For historical context, see Bernard-Henri Lévy, *The Genius of Judaism*, trans. Steven B. Kennedy (New York: Random House, 2017), 140. According to Lévy, the contemporaneous king of Nineveh, Tiglath-Pileser III, had already captured part of the Northern Kingdom and had taken its inhabitants into exile. Therefore, Jonah has good reason to be scared of going to this great enemy city, and God's command to Jonah to tell the city that it will be destroyed lest they change their behavior may have had geopolitical and not just moral valences to it.

10   Abarbanel on Jonah 1:3.

11   Abarbanel on Jonah 1:5.

12   *Vayikra Rabbah* 4:6.

13   The Book of Job is the only other book in the Hebrew Bible that concerns itself almost exclusively with non-Jews.

14 Academics generally identify the biblical town of Nineveh in the
    Assyrian Empire as modern-day Mosul, Iraq, on the eastern bank
    of the Tigris River. By the time the Bible was canonized, Nineveh no
    longer existed. However, it remained residually in the biblical imagi-
    nation as a mythic city of great proportions, capable of great evil but
    also capable of great and rapid change. See Erica Brown, *Jonah: The
    Reluctant Prophet* (Jerusalem: Maggid Books, 2017), xxvii–xxviii.
15 *Babylonian Talmud, M'gilah* 31a.
16 *Jerusalem Talmud, Gittin* 5:5; *Babylonian Talmud, Ta'anit* 16a.
17 *Tosefta, Bava Kama* 10:5.
18 *B'reishit Rabbah* 3:9.
19 Avivah Gottlieb Zornberg, *The Murmuring Deep: Reflections on the
    Biblical Unconscious* (New York: Schocken Books, 2009), 83.
20 Part of the appeal of the book for Christians is that it is typological and
    foreshadows events found in the New Testament. For example, in the
    Gospels of Matthew (12:39–41) and Luke (11:31–32), Jonah represents
    Jesus. Jesus spends three days in the grave, as Jonah spends three
    days in the fish. Further, it is suggested that Jesus lives in a corrupt
    Nineveh-like culture but one that will not repent yet as it did for
    Jonah.
21 See the writings, for example, of Jerome, Augustine of Hippo,
    and Theodore of Mopsuestia. Furthermore: "The Church fathers
    accepted the Jewish interpretation but turned it against its authors.
    Theodore of Mopsuestia says Jonah was sent to Nineveh because the
    Jews refused to listen to the prophets, and the book about Jonah was
    written to teach a lesson to the stiff-necked people. Nineveh believed,
    says Jerome, but incredulous Israel persists in refusing to acknowl-
    edge Jesus" (Elias Bickerman, *Four Strange Books of the Bible: Jonah,
    Daniel, Koheleth, Esther* [New York: Schocken Books, 1985], 16).
22 They also suggested that this story somehow serves as proof for how
    negatively Jews perceive gentiles. See James D. Smart, *The Interpreter's
    Bible* (Nashville: Abingdon: 1956), 6:871.
23 "It has become customary to see Jonah as a petty, narrow-minded and
    stiff-necked representative of his stubborn people, and anti-Semites
    have always found in this book a fertile ground for their poisonous
    seeds" (Andre Lacocque and Pierre-Emmanuel Lacocque, *The Jonah
    Complex* [Atlanta: John Knox Press, 1981], 4).
24 Lacocque and Lacocque, *Jonah Complex*, 24.
25 Radak on Jonah 1:1.
26 Brown, *Jonah*, xvii.
27 *Babylonian Talmud, Eruvin* 96a.

28 *Pirkei D'Rabbi Eliezer* 33.
29 *Pirkei D'Rabbi Eliezer* 33; *Jerusalem Talmud, Sukkah* 5.
30 The scholar George Landes argues that the Book of Jonah has "no fewer than 63 places in the text where the author's deliberate or inadvertent withholding of information poses at least some interpretive issue of for the reader and, in addition, 13 places where narrative features create a dissonance in the logic or coherence of the story" (George M. Landes, "Textual 'Information Gaps' and 'Dissonances' in the Interpretation of the Book of Jonah," in *Ki Baruch Hu: Ancient Near Eastern, Biblical, and Judaic Studies in Honor of Baruch A. Levine*, ed. William W. Hallo, Lawrence H. Schiffman, and Robert Chazan [Winona Lake, IN: Eisenbrauns, 1999], 273–74).
31 Brown, *Jonah*, xxi–xxii.
32 Diane E. Holloway, *Analyzing Leaders, Presidents and Terrorists* (New York: Writer's Club Press, 2002), 168.
33 Jonathan Sacks, *Lessons in Leadership* (Jerusalem: Maggid, 2015), 138.

CHAPTER I

34 James Ackerman, "Jonah," in *The Literary Guide to the Bible*, ed. Robert Alter and Frank Kermode (Cambridge, MA: Harvard University Press, 1987), 234.
35 This wickedness is later described as *chamas* ("violence"), just as in the Flood story found in Genesis.
36 Nineveh gets built as a great city in Genesis 10:10–12.
37 Except when protesting is a risk to life, health, or safety.
38 While this verse calls on everyone to rebuke, *Babylonian Talmud, Shabbat* 55a suggests that it is the responsibility of leaders to rebuke: "Let the Master rebuke."
39 Maimonides, *Mishneh Torah, Hilchot Dei'ot* 6:7.
40 The morning service: *Shacharit*.
41 *Babylonian Talmud, B'rachot* 26b.
42 See Abraham Joshua Heschel, "A Prayer for Peace," in *Moral Grandeur and Spiritual Audacity: Essays*, ed. Susannah Heschel (New York: Farrar, Strauss and Giroux, 1996), 231.
43 *Babylonian Talmud, Shabbat* 54b.
44 On the other hand, the rabbis were also aware that not everyone could engage in this line of work effectively. See *Babylonian Talmud, Y'vamot* 65b: "Just as there is a mitzvah for a person to say words (of rebuke) that will be accepted, so too there is a mitzvah for a person not to say words (of rebuke) that will not be accepted."
45 *Sh'mot Rabbah* 27:9.

46 "Why We Went: A Joint Letter from the Rabbis Arrested in St. Augustine" (1964), in *Studies in the Meaning of Judaism*, by Eugene B. Borowitz (Philadelphia: Jewish Publication Society, 2002), 90.

47 I speak here mainly about white Jews who have benefited from skin color and class privilege in the United States. Jews of color, LBGTQ Jews, working-class or poor Jews, Jewish recent immigrants, and disabled/differently abled Jews are not generally afforded "insider" status.

48 *Babylonian Talmud, Sanhedrin* 73a.

49 See *P'sikta D'Rav Kahana* 12:6.

50 Rabbi Yitzchak Hutner comments about the parallel between Purim and Yom Kippur: "The Vilna Gaon wrote: Here is a rule for every *yom tov*, that it is half for God and half for you. Two holidays are exceptions to this rule. Yom Kippur is entirely for God, and Purim is entirely for you. But . . . there is no exception from the rule. For Yom Kippurim is Yom K-("like")-Purim. Meaning: both together make up one holy time. And in this holy time are included Purim and Yom Kippur, and it stands as half for God and half for you" (*Pachad Yitzchak*, Purim 8). Further, consider the parallel of the casting lots in Jonah 1:7 and Esther 3:7.

51 Nahum Sarna, *Understanding Genesis: The World of the Bible in the Light of History* (New York: Schocken Books, 1970), 145–46.

52 We might ask ourselves about how we run away from God today. Do we run from moral responsibility? Do we run from silence and spiritual engagement? Do we run from our mortality? Do we avoid addressing big theological questions? Indeed, it is only human to hide.

CHAPTER 2

53 The extended love poem known as the Song of Songs, which may be a metaphor for God's love of Israel, frequently returns to the idea of hiding from obligation.

54 Robert Alter, *Strong as Love Is Death* (New York: Norton, 2015), 139.

55 Ibn Ezra on Jonah 1:1.

56 Joseph Campbell, *The Hero with a Thousand Faces* (Novato, CA: New World Library, 2008), 49.

57 It is interesting to consider this point in light of the postmodern notions of moral relativism and our inability to critique other cultures for their moral norms. Should we promote universal morality or cultural relativism?

58 Blank, *Understanding the Prophets*, 45.

59 Estimated to be a population of 120,000 according to Jonah 4:11.

60 *B'reishit Rabbah* 8:5.
61 Emmanuel Levinas, "On Jewish Philosophy" (1985), in *Is It Righteous To Be? Interviews with Emmanuel Levinas*, ed. Jill Robbins (Stanford, CA: Stanford University Press, 2001), 243.
62 Abraham Isaac Kook, *Notebook* 8:429, 1919.
63 Nachmanides on Exodus 3:2.
64 Rabbi Abraham Joshua Heschel (in *Who Is Man?*) refers to this emotion as "radical amazement."
65 Michael Fishbane, *Sacred Attunement: A Jewish Theology* (Chicago: University of Chicago Press, 2008), 279.
66 *Hineini* is the response sometimes given to a divine call, such as by Abraham (Genesis 22:1) and Moses (Exodus 3:4).
67 Jonathan Sacks, *To Heal a Fractured World: The Ethics of Responsibility* (New York: Schocken Books, 2005), 262.
68 Evidence for this claim can be discerned within the Book of Jonah primarily in the fact that God performs miracles for Jonah. Furthermore, Jonah is a direct student of the prophet Elisha (Rashi on I Kings 9:1). The mystical commentary found in the *Zohar* states that "Jonah arrives from the strength of (the prophet) Elijah (Commentary on Exodus, 193).
69 Spinoza, *Ethics* (1677), part III, definition 13: explanation.
70 Rosa Parks with Gregory J. Reed, *Quiet Strength: The Faith, the Hope, and the Heart of a Woman Who Changed a Nation* (Grand Rapids, MI: Zondervan, 1994), 17.
71 I Kings 10:21–22; Ezekiel 27:12.
72 For an alternative view, Rashi, in his commentary on Jonah 1:3, suggests that Tarshish is not a city but a sea. This suggests that Jonah isn't actually aiming to get anywhere, but merely to get out of here. Yitzhak Berger suggests that Jonah is seeking the Garden of Eden and that Tarshish is "a kind of mythic paradise, replete with abundant riches" and that he is so distressed over the *kikayon* plant withering because it "embodies an Edenic-domain" that he truly seeks. See Yitzhak Berger, *Jonah in the Shadows of Eden* (Bloomington: Indiana University Press, 2016), 3.
73 James Ackerman, "Jonah," in *The Literary Guide to the Bible*, 235.
74 Ernest Becker, *The Denial of Death* (New York: Free Press, 1973), 27.
75 *B'reishit Rabbah* 32:11.
76 Becker, *Denial of Death*, 2.
77 The alternative is quite dangerous. Jonah became so convinced that he must hide that the only alternative he could fathom was death. Multiple times he requests death instead of coming out of hiding.

CHAPTER 3

78 *Pirkei D'Rabbi Eliezer* 10.

79 To be sure, we now are becoming aware of just how much humanity has influenced nature through the waste and pollution produced by unregulated capitalism.

80 Yochanan Muffs, *The Personhood of God: Biblical Theology, Human Faith, and the Divine Image* (Woodstock, VT: Jewish Lights, 2005), 184.

81 Jonah 1:5. Maybe we read the Book of Jonah on Yom Kippur so that it reminds us to wake up from our slumber—to be like the sailors, and not like Jonah.

82 Steven Bob, trans., *Go to Nineveh: Medieval Jewish Commentaries on the Book of Jonah, Translated and Explained* (Eugene, OR: Pickwick, 2013), 145.

CHAPTER 4

83 Maimonides, *Sh'monah P'rakim, Hakdamah*.

84 Maimonides, *Sh'monah P'rakim, Hakdamah*.

85 Rashi on Jonah 1:5, based on *Pirkei D'Rabbi Eliezer* 10, shares that each person on the boat had a different god and that every nationality was present on this ship. Jonah's was the quintessential universalistic journey.

86 Peter Berger and Anton Zijderveld, *In Praise of Doubt: How to Have Convictions without Becoming a Fanatic* (New York: Harper One, 2009), 7.

87 Irving (Yitz) Greenberg, *For the Sake of Heaven and Earth: The New Encounter between Judaism and Christianity* (Philadelphia: Jewish Publication Society, 2004), 196.

88 Nathan T. Lopes Cardozo, *Crisis, Covenant, and Creativity* (Jerusalem: Urim, 2004), p. 38.

89 See *Babylonian Talmud, Kiddushin* 31a.

90 This concept is called *chasidei umot ha'olam*. See *Mishneh Torah, Hilchot M'lachim Umilchamot* 8:11.

91 Maimonides, *Mishneh Torah, Hilchot M'lachim Umilchamot* 11.

92 Jonathan Sacks, *The Dignity of Difference: How to Avoid the Clash of Civilizations* (New York: Continuum, 2003), 20.

93 Joseph B. Soloveitchik, "Confrontation," *Tradition: A Journal of Orthodox Thought* 6, no. 2 (1964): 17.

94 See Lenn E. Goodman, *Religious Pluralism and Values in the Public Sphere* (New York: Cambridge University Press, 2014), 28.

CHAPTER 5

95 Indeed, they appear to attempt to prevent throwing him overboard. These sailors are the heroes of this chapter, doing all they can to save Jonah's life, albeit while suspecting he is the one responsible. *Pirkei D'Rabbi Eliezer* suggests that they saw other ships next to them not at all affected by the storm, indicating that their predicament was due to someone on their ship .

96 According to a *midrash*, the sailors "took Jonah and lowered him up to his knees into the ocean, and the sea quieted from its storm. But when they drew him back, the sea raged again. So they lowered him until his navel, and the sea's storm grew still; but when they lifted him out, it raged again. They lowered him up to his neck, and the sea quieted; but again, as soon as they had raised him, it raged. Finally, they lowered Jonah's entire body into the ocean. Immediately, the storm at sea ceased." See David Stern's translation in "Jonah and the Sailors from *Pirkei D'Rabbi Eliezer*," in *Rabbinic Fantasies: Imaginative Narratives from Classical Hebrew Literature* (New Haven: Yale University Press, 1998), 64.

97 Rabbi Jonathan Magonet shows that there are symmetries in the Book of Jonah: in chapters 1 and 3, Jonah encounters others (sailors, Nineveh), whereas in chapters 2 and 4, Jonah is alone with God (praying or debating), and his prayer and God's response in chapter 4 get equal time. The book is a mix between exploring social dynamics and exploring the existential nature of the inner world.

98 "Suicide," National Institute of Mental Health, accessed February 26, 2019, https://www.nimh.nih.gov/health/statistics/suicide.shtml.

99 Nell Greenfieldboyce, "CDC: U.S. Suicide Rates Have Climbed Dramatically," NPR, June 7, 2018, https://www.npr.org/sections/health-shots/2018/06/07/617897261/cdc-u-s-suicide-rates-have-climbed-dramatically.

100 *Babylonian Talmud, Avodah Zarah* 18a.

101 *Minor Tractate S'machot* 2:4–5, critical edition by Rabbi Dr. Michael Higger (1931).

102 The Talmud is trying to identify the minimum amount of pain that can be considered to be suffering.

103 *Babylonian Talmud, Arachin* 16b.

104 *S'machot* 2:1–3 through *Chatam Sofer* on *Yoreih Dei'ah* 326.

105 *Aruch Hashulchan, Yoreih Dei'ah* 345.

106 Uriel Simon, *Mikra LeYisrael: Ovadia Yona* (Tel Aviv: Am Oved / Magnes Press, 1992), 48.

107 *Malachim* is replaced with *anashim* in Jonah 1:10, 1:13, and 1:16.

108 "Because the Hebrew Bible's aural quality was important, particularly in the days before mass printing and universal literacy, a listener to this story would have heard the term and perhaps made the association that the sailors were indeed angels in the way they treated Jonah and in their leading questions which created a forced self-reflection for someone fleeing and sleeping" (Brown, *Jonah*, 40).

109 For more of my thoughts on this topic, see my analysis of *Pirkei Avot* 4:4 in *Pirkei Avot: A Social Justice Commentary* (New York: CCAR Press, 2018), 202–4.

CHAPTER 6

110 Dominion is morally justifiable when humans guard and protect other animals. Consumption, however, is a point of significant moral debate. There is no moral debate about abuse though, which all agree is wrong.

111 Fascinatingly, the rabbis imagine that Jonah, in his arrogance, takes credit for saving the fish rather than expressing gratitude for his own salvation: "Jonah then said to the fish, 'See! I have saved you from the mouth of Leviathan. Now show me everything in the depths of the ocean'" (*Pirkei D'Rabbi Eliezer* 10). This remarkable *midrash* then turns the fish into a time-traveling machine, giving Jonah the tour of a lifetime.

112 "Rabbi Tarfon commented: The fish that swallowed Jonah had been assigned this task since the six days of Creation, as it is said, 'The Eternal provided a huge fish to swallow Jonah' (Jonah 21:1). Jonah entered its mouth the way a man enters a large synagogue. He stood there and the eyes of the fish shone down upon him like two skylights." See the translation of *Pirkei D'Rabbi Eliezer* by David Stern and Mark Jay Mirsky: "Jonah and the Sailors from *Pirkei d'Rabbi Eliezer*," in *Rabbinic Fantasies: Imaginative Narratives from Classical Hebrew Literature* (New Haven, CT: Yale University Press, 1998), 64.

113 Although, there most certainly are ethical pescatarians (those who choose not to eat land animals but will eat fish).

114 Maimonides, *Guide for the Perplexed* 3:13.

115 Deuteronomy 22:6. See also *Babylonian Talmud, Chulin* 140b; *Babylonian Talmud, Kiddushin* 39b.

116 *Babylonian Talmud, Bava M'tzi'a* 32b.

117 *Sh'mot Rabbah* 2:2.

118 *Babylonian Talmud, B'rachot* 40a.

119 For a more in-depth analysis of this shift and how these verses have been interpreted, see Rabbi Shai Held's guided source sheet "Is

Vegetarianism an Ideal for Jews?," Hadar, Winter 2014, https://www.hadar.org/torah-resource/vegetarianism-ideal-jews.

120 *Babylonian Talmud, Sanhedrin* 59b.

121 Albo, *Sefer Ha'ikarim*, vol. 3, chapter 15; and Abarbanel on Exodus 16:4.

122 *Babylonian Talmud, Chulin* 84a.

123 The butterfly effect is a concept that is understood in popular culture as the idea that tiny occurrences have significant, unforeseen impacts. The scientists who developed this concept intended it to mean that small variations in conditions can have large, unpredictable results (James Vernon, *American Scientist* 105, no. 3 [May–June 2017]: 130). Understood either way, the point is that the world is a web of interconnected causes and effects.

124 Radak on Jonah 4:11.

125 Erica Brown, *Seder Talk: The Conversational Haggada* (Jerusalem: Koren, 2015), 61.

126 *Jerusalem Talmud, Ta'anit* 2:3.

127 Theodor H. Gaster, *Myth, Legend, and Custom in the Old Testament* (New York: Harper & Row, 1969), 655–56.

128 *Babylonian Talmud, Beitzah* 32b.

CHAPTER 7

129 This is one of the great challenges of using set prayer books. We do not *write* our prayers.

130 Brown, *Jonah*, 111.

131 The Mahari Kra (Rabbi Joseph ben Simon Kara, ca. 1060–1135) on Jonah 2:10 suggests that this may have been *Birkat Hagomel*. According to the Talmud, the blessing of *hagomel* is traditionally recited by four types of individuals who experienced a miraculous salvation: one who crosses the desert, one who is healed from sickness, one who is freed from prison, and one who completes a sea voyage (*Babylonian Talmud, B'rachot* 54b). Today, many continue to *bench gomel* after returning from travels overseas. Some women recite this blessing after safely giving birth.

132 *Mishnah B'rachot* 9:3.

133 Notations from the *Vaad* (4–5), 153.

134 *Vayikra Rabbah* 7:2.

135 See also Chris Harrison, "3 Steps to Hitbodedut: Talking to God on Your Own Terms," ReformJudaism.org, August 27, 2019, https://reformjudaism.org/practice/spirituality/3-steps-hitbodedut-talking-god-your-own-terms.

136 Maimonides, *Mishneh Torah, Hilchot T'filah* 1.

137 *Nachmanides* on *Sefer Hamitzvot*, #5.

138 Abraham R. Besdin, *Reflections of the Rav*, vol. 1 (Hoboken, NJ: Ktav, 1979), 80–81.

139 Maimonides, *Guide for the Perplexed* 3:28.

140 Maimonides, *Guide for the Perplexed* 3:36.

141 Maimonides, *Guide for the Perplexed* 3:35 and 3:44.

142 *Mishnah B'rachot* 9:3.

143 Hara Person, "Rosh HaShanah in the Pines," 2015/5776, *Fact/Fiction*, September 10, 2015, http://haraperson.com/2015/09/rosh-hashanah-in-the-pines-2015/.

144 Ibn Ezra on Jonah 1:15.

145 Zornberg, *The Murmuring Deep*, 104.

CHAPTER 8

146 *B'reishit Rabbah* 56:1.

147 Malbim on Jonah 2:1.

148 The text is quite clear that the people of Nineveh repent, while the rabbis debate the extent of the repentance (*Mishnah Gittin* 5:5; *Babylonian Talmud, Ta'anit* 16a). But the extent of Jonah's repentance is unclear.

149 Even though the people of Nineveh must suspect that Jonah is a prophet if they heard about his salvation in the sea, we still learn that they did not repent because of their belief in him. Rather, it says in Jonah that "the people of Nineveh believed in God." This seems to be teaching that no matter the strength of one's prophecy or the charisma of the leader, even a prophet, we seek to follow God and absolute truth rather than leaders.

150 Maimonides, *Mishneh Torah, Hilchot T'shuvah* 1–2.

151 Rabbinic imagination suggests that the king of Nineveh was none other than Pharaoh himself! This might explain why the city of Nineveh seems to repent so quickly. Pharaoh remembers what it was like to disobey God. Perhaps he was testing God to see if in this new era, God was still present and responding. Only the slightest reminder was enough to call the city to repent. Who else, the rabbis imagine, could understand so quickly? Indeed, it is understood that repentance is difficult for all of us.

152 For psychological readings of the Book of Jonah, Dr. Erica Brown recommends these sources: Bruno Bettelheim, *The Uses of Enchantment* (New York: Knopf, 1976); Hyman Fingert's strange interpretation in "The Psychoanalytical Study of the Minor Prophet Jonah," *Psychoanalytic Review* 41 (1954): 55–65; Joseph More, "The Prophet Jonah: The Story of an Intrapsychic Process," *American Imago* 27 (1970): 3–11; and

Erich Fromm, *The Forgotten Language* (New York: Grove Press, 1937), 22.

153 *Babylonian Talmud, Eruvin* 19a.

154 Rashi on Jonah 2:3.

155 *Babylonian Talmud, Bava Batra* 73b compares exile to a large fish.

CHAPTER 9

156 Craig Haney, "Mental Health Issues in Long-Term Solitary and 'Supermax' Confinement," *Crime and Delinquency* 49, no. 1 (January 2003).

157 Haney, "Mental Health Issues."

158 Haney, "Mental Health Issues."

159 More than a decade ago, clinicians working on the issue created a term for this condition: special housing unit (SHU) syndrome. Those with SHU syndrome were considered to have the following symptoms:
     • A predilection toward paranoia and insomnia
     • Distorted perception of time
     • Heightened feelings of inner rage and fear
     • Increased suicidal tendencies
     See Jason M. Breslow, "What Does Solitary Confinement Do to Your Mind?," *Frontline*, PBS, April 22, 2014, https://www.pbs.org/wgbh/frontline/article/what-does-solitary-confinement-do-to-your-mind/.

160 Sarah Baumgartel, Corey Guilmette, Johanna Kalb, Diana Li, Joshua Nuni, Devon Porter, and Judith Resnik, "Time-In-Cell: The ASCA-Liman 2014 National Survey of Administrative Segregation in Prison," Yale Law School, Public Law Research Paper No. 552, August 2, 2015, https://ssrn.com/abstract=2655627 or http://dx.doi.org/10.2139/ssrn.2655627.

161 Almost 90 percent of inmates in solitary confinement cultivate further challenges with "irrational anger," as compared to just 3 percent of the general population. Scholars have attributed this to the extended absence of any opportunities for happiness or joy.

162 For an alternative view to this common belief that *tzara'at* is the result of sin, see Dr. Amit Gvaryahu, "Thoughts on Parashat Tazria-Metzora," Drisha Institute of Jewish Education, May 8, 2013, https://www.youtube.com/watch?v=kEdjFLJ3R1Y.

163 The resulting work is called the *Septuagint.* According to rabbinic tradition, although each of the seventy-two rabbis instructed to translate the Bible into Greek was held in solitary confinement, each of the seventy-two resulting translations was identical to all the others (*Babylonian Talmud, M'gilah* 9a).

164 Barack H. Obama, "Barack Obama: Why We Must Rethink Solitary

Confinement," *Washington Post*, January 25, 2016, https://www. washingtonpost.com/opinions/barack-obama-why-we-must-rethink-solitary-confinement/2016/01/25/29a361f2-c384-11e5-8965-0607e0e265ce_story.html?utm_term=.ebf359c0a30c.

165 This verse is often read to mean that God created humans of two genders because of the human need to be helped by others. I suggest a broader reading here: the need to share the human experience with other human beings goes beyond a need for interaction between and among those with different genders and gender identities.

166 *Babylonian Talmud, Ta'anit* 23a.

167 See, for example, Jane E. Brody, "The Surprising Effects of Loneliness on Health," *New York Times*, December 11, 2017, https://www. nytimes.com/2017/12/11/well/mind/how-loneliness-affects-our-health.html.

168 *Babylonian Talmud, Sanhedrin* 98a.

169 Diane Swanbrow, "Compassion: College Students Do Not Have as Much as They Used To," *University of Michigan News*, January 15, 2019, https://news.umich.edu/ compassion-college-students-don-t-have-as-much-as-they-used-to/.

CHAPTER 10

170 Rashi on Jonah 2:1; also see Ibn Ezra on Jonah 2:2.

171 One mystical approach suggests that the fish died as soon as Jonah entered and was only revived at the end of the three days (*Zohar, Parshat Vayak'hel*).

172 Mary Daly, *Beyond God the Father: Toward a Philosophy of Women's Liberation* (Boston: Beacon Press, 1973), 19.

173 Song of Songs, for example.

174 The problem is more acute in the Hebrew language, where the language is gendered, without the alternative options that we can find so readily in English.

175 *Mishnah, Sanhedrin* 4:5.

176 *Jerusalem Talmud, N'darim* 9:41.

CHAPTER 11

177 *Pirkei D'Rabbi Eliezer* suggests that Noah built the ark for fifty-two years, providing more than ample time to engage others. To be sure, one *midrash* (*Tanchuma, Noach* 5) suggests that Noah worked on the project for decades precisely to give others the chance to repent. Most commentators, however, agree that Noah did not care at all about saving his generation (*Babylonian Talmud, Sanhedrin* 108a; *Pirkei D'Rabbi*

Eliezer 22; *B'reishit Rabbah* 30:7; *Vayikra Rabbah* 27:5).

178 Rabbi Steven Bob, *Go to Nineveh*, 143.

179 The storm that rocked the boat of Jonah and the sailors is known as one of the greatest storms in the *Tanach* (*Kohelet Rabbah* 1:6).

180 Judy Klitsner, *Subversive Sequels in the Bible: How Biblical Stories Mine and Undermine Each Other* (Jerusalem: Maggid Books, 2011), 10.

181 Klitsner, *Subversive Sequels in the Bible*, 2.

182 Klitsner, *Subversive Sequels in the Bible*, 20.

183 *B'reishit Rabbah* 30:7. Indeed, in another *midrash*, the rabbis are troubled that no warning was given before the Flood, and so they interpret "Make yourself an ark of gopher wood" (Genesis 6:14) to mean that Noah made clear to the people what was happening (*Tanchuma, Noach*): Noah was instructed not to cut down already existing trees for the construction of the ark, but to plant new trees to give the people time to learn and to adapt. Other commentators take different views of Noah's virtues and vices in this story.

184 Brown, *Jonah*, 139.

185 See also Psalm 145:9: "The Eternal is good to all and God's mercy is upon all God's works."

CHAPTER 12

186 Rashi on Jonah 3:4. To support this reading, consider Psalm 30:12 and Lamentations 5:15.

187 Rashi on Genesis 18:21, citing *Babylonian Talmud, Sanhedrin* 109b.

188 *Babylonian Talmud, Sanhedrin* 108a.

189 Radak on Jonah 1:2 and 3:8.

190 Abarbanel on Jonah 3:10.

191 *Pirkei Avot* 2:4.

192 *Babylonian Talmud, B'rachot* 5a.

193 Some people might fall into the opposite extreme and be so hard upon themselves that they only know how to be hard on others as well. In both cases, we must return gently and forcefully to our own growth.

CHAPTER 13

194 *Babylonian Talmud, M'gilah* 31a. Jonah is read during the *Ne'ilah* service, the prayers that close Yom Kippur and inspire especially high spiritual fervor.

195 Ibn Ezra on Jonah 1:2.

196 Abarbanel on Jonah 4:1.

197 It is worth noting that the notion of "judgment" in theology is not so appealing to modern people. This may be precisely the point. We can

engage in the High Holy Days with a spirit of love rather than a spirit of judgment. That is what God is teaching us in the Book of Jonah.

198 Abraham Joshua Heschel, *The Prophets* (New York: Perennial, 2001), 4.

199 Heschel, *Moral Grandeur and Spiritual Audacity*, 292.

CHAPTER 14

200 Brown, *Jonah*, xiii–xiv.

201 Joseph Campbell, *Reflections on the Art of Living: A Joseph Campbell Companion*, ed. Diane K. Osbon (New York: Harper Perennial, 1995), 18.

202 On this matter, Erica Brown writes, "Arguably, Jonah had been dying since his very first appearance, with this suicidal mission to flee from God, to descend into the bowels of a ship in the midst of capsizing and then, finally, with this request for the sailors to throw him overboard" (Brown, *Jonah*, 114).

203 Abraham Isaac Kook, *Orot Hakodesh*, 3:270.

204 John Dewey, *Human Nature and Conduct: An Introduction to Social Psychology* (New York: Henry Holt, 1922), 238, 241–42.

205 Brown, *Jonah*, 53.

206 Oliver Wendell Holmes, *New York Trust Co. v. Eisner*, 256 U.S. 345, 349 (1921).

207 Heschel, *The Prophets*, 368.

CHAPTER 15

208 Of course, there are also nonreligious fundamentalists, but the most pervasive and destructive contemporary kind of fundamentalism is religious fundamentalism.

209 Barack Obama, *The Audacity of Hope* (New York: Crown, 2006), 55.

210 *Sh'mot Rabbah* 31:15.

211 *Yalkut Shimoni* on Genesis 1:13.

212 In recent years, people have been murdered over this issue.

213 Sacks, *The Dignity of Difference*, 10, 20.

214 Sacks, *The Dignity of Difference*, 50, 53.

215 Of course, there are Jewish fundamentalist and extremists today, too. Consider, as just one example, the Pride march in Jerusalem 2015, where one of the marchers was murdered and five others were severely wounded by fundamentalist Yishai Schlissel.

216 Unfortunately, Akbar's experiment died with him.

217 See Gandhi, *Collected Works*, vol. 40 (New Delhi: Government of India, 1929), 60.

218 Brown, *Seder Talk*, 36.

CHAPTER 16

219 Rashi on Exodus 32:10.
220 Kook, *Orot Hakodesh* 4e.

CHAPTER 17

221 Rashi on Deuteronomy 30:3.
222 Ibn Pakuda's most well-known book, written originally in Arabic, is frequently translated as *Chovot Halevavot*, literally "Duties of the Hearts."
223 Abraham Isaac Kook, *Olat Ra'ayah*, 1:330.
224 Of course, there are different theological views within Judaism and even within the interpretations of this Chasidic idea.
225 The term *tikkun olam* is used in multiple ways in Jewish thought. The Talmud uses the term to describe a policy of rabbinic legislation in commerce and family law. *Tikkun olam* as a kabbalistic concept relates to our call to repair elements of the world that were damaged in the course of the creation of the world. And in the twentieth and twenty-first centuries, the phrase has been understood as describing our obligation to take affirmative steps to make the world a better place. While some have criticized this latter use of the term as an ignorant adaptation of an unrelated term, I would argue that specific biblical and rabbinic statements and an overall understanding of Jewish thought and Jewish values support the idea that this view of *tikkun olam* stands at the core of Judaism.
226 Abarbanel, commentary on Jonah 3:4, based on "My heart has turned over within me" (Lamentations 1:20).
227 Brown, *Jonah*, 143–44.
228 Jeffrey Tigay: "Under this conception the job of prophecy seems simple: Speak what God tells you and you will always be proved right. History is intelligible, God's word always comes to pass, and the prophet is a celebrity. But how tragic is the new conception! Speak what God tells you, but speak it so effectively that the people will be moved to change their ways and thus obviate your dire prediction (cf. Jer. 26:18–19). If your reputation suffers in the process—that's a small price to pay for what you will have accomplished!" Jeffrey Tigay, "The Book of Jonah and the Days of Awe," *Conservative Judaism* 38, no. 2 (Winter 1985–86): 67–76.
229 Ibn Ezra commentary on Jonah 1:2.
230 *Tanchuma* on Leviticus 8.
231 *Mei Hashilo'ach*, vol. 2, Prophets, Jonah 4:1.
232 To be sure, climate change is but one reason for the pending mass

extinction. Human expansion into the animals' natural habitat, chemical pollution, and overhunting and overfishing are other reasons. Those are all human-made problems.

CHAPTER 19

233 James Kugel, *How to Read the Bible: A Guide to Scripture Then and Now* (New York: Free Press, 2007), 628–29.

234 Rashi on Jonah 2:6.

235 See Bobby L. Lovett, *The Civil Rights Movement in Tennessee: A Narrative History* (Knoxville: University of Tennessee Press, 2005), 220.

236 *Babylonian Talmud, N'darim* 38a.

237 Radak on Jonah 1:3.

238 *D'rashot HaRan*, sermon 5.

239 Maimonides, *Guide for the Perplexed* 2:32. Also, *Mishneh Torah, Yesodei HaTorah* 7. Also see *Sh'monah P'rakim*.

240 Maimonides understood that the sages merely explore an abstract concept rather than issuing a hard rule to be applied universally. Individual teachings in the Talmud are generally not to be understood as applying to all cases and situations. They can be what Rabbi Dr. Yitz Greenberg described as "moment truths," meaning that all truths last temporarily, some longer than others.

241 Abarbanel on *Guide for the Perplexed* 2:32.

242 Consider how Amos (7:10–15) spoke out against the sins of the rich king Jeroboam II. He told him that he would not sell his prophecies for cash. Having financial independence helped him to maintain his prophetic integrity.

243 This would be similar to the idea that judges were required to have financial independence (*Babylonian Talmud, Sanhedrin* 7b) and the provision of the United States Constitution that provides lifetime tenure to federal judges. Federalist No. 78, http://avalon.law.yale.edu/18th_century/fed78.asp.

244 The Chasidic master Rebbe Nachman (late eighteenth century, Ukraine), not a person of means, understands the role of wealth (*Likutei Moharan* 60:1) and *ta'avat mamon* ("lustful desire for money") to be of the most spiritually debilitating desires.

245 See the opinions of Rabbi David Kimchi and Nissim of Gerona.

246 *Jerusalem Talmud, Sukkah* 5:1.

CHAPTER 20

247 Zvi Grumet, *Genesis: From Creation to Covenant* (Jerusalem: Maggid Books, 2017), 86–87.

248 Chofetz Chayim, *Sha'ar Hatziyun* 622:6.
249 See Edward Hoffman, *The Kabbalah Reader: A Sourcebook of Visionary Judaism* (Boston: Trumpeter, 2010), 126–27.
250 The theological field examining the religious problem of why the righteous can suffer and why the wicked can prosper.
251 Rabbi Chayim ben Moshe Ibn Attar, *Or Hachayim* (1696–1743, Morocco and Jerusalem) on Genesis 1:26.

CHAPTER 21

252 Relying on 1993 data, the United States Geological Survey reports that about 71 percent of the earth's surface is water-covered (https://www.usgs.gov/media/images/distribution-water-and-above-earth). That same agency reports that the percentage of human body composition consisting of water varies from about 55 percent to about 78 percent depending on a person's sex and age (https://www.usgs.gov/special-topic/water-science-school/science/water-you-water-and-human-body?qt-science_center_objects=0#qt-science_center_objects).
253 Concerning the deadliness of water, see Isaiah 55:1; *Babylonian Talmud, Bava Kama* 82a.
254 The World Health Organization reports that as of 2015 over half a billion people on the planet did not have access to clean, safe drinking water (https://www.who.int/news-room/fact-sheets/detail/drinking-water). Polluted, contaminated water is a major global crisis. Also, due to climate change, we will witness an increased level of deadly droughts and floods (Union of Concerned Scientists, Fact Sheet: "The Science Connecting Extreme Weather to Climate Change," June 2018, https://www.ucsusa.org/sites/default/files/attach/2018/06/The-Science-Connecting-Extreme-Weather-to-Climate-Change.pdf; Center for Climate and Energy Solutions, "Drought and Climate Change," May 9, 2019, https://www.c2es.org/content/drought-and-climate-change/).
255 See, for example, Exodus 29; Leviticus 1–7, 11–15; Numbers 19.
256 Based on Micah 7:19, "And You will hurl [*v'tashlich*] all our sins into the depths of the sea."
257 *Babylonian Talmud, Ta'anit* 9a.
258 *Babylonian Talmud, Kiddushin* 29a.
259 In addition to engaging in ritual to raise our awareness and elevate our spiritual consciousness, we might contemplate our personal water usage and our monthly water bill and consider various approaches to water conservation.

CHAPTER 22

260 *Qur'an, surah* 37:139–148.

261 *Qur'an, surah* 21:87 and *surah* 68:48.

262 Sahih al-Bukhari, 4:55:608.

263 Stephen J. Vicchio, *Biblical Figures in the Islamic Faith* (Eugene, OR: Wipf & Stock, 2008), 74.

264 Nineveh officials later confirmed that the desecrated monument was identified as the Tomb of Jonah.

265 Some have even suggested that Maimonides converted to Islam at one point, albeit probably via religious coercion. See Norman Stillman, "The Jewish Experience in the Muslim World," in *The Cambridge Guide to Jewish, History, Religion, and Culture*, ed. Judith Baskin and Kenneth Seeskin (New York: Cambridge University Press 2010), 106. Also see Joel Kramer, *Maimonides: The Life and World of One of Civilization's Greatest Minds* (New York: Doubleday, 2008).

266 Maimonides, *Responsa* 448.

267 See Maimonides, *Ethical Writings of* Maimonides, ed. Raymond L. Weiss and Charles Butterworth (New York: Dover, 1975), 173.

268 David Rosen, "Jewish Approaches to Dialogue, IJCIC-WCC Meetings, London, October 14–16, 2012," Davidrosen.net, accessed May 28, 2019, https://www.rabbidavidrosen.net/wp-content/uploads/2016/02/Jewish_approaches_to_dialogue_IJCIC-WCC_meeting_London_October_2012.pdf.

CHAPTER 23

269 Abraham Maslow, *The Farther Reaches of Human Nature* (New York: Viking Press, 1971), 35.

270 Maharal, *Tiferet Yisrael.*

271 James W. Fowler, *Stages of Faith: The Psychology of Human Development and the Quest for Meaning* (New York: Harper One, 1981), 201.

272 *Babylonian Talmud, Avodah Zarah* 19a.

273 Joseph B. Soloveitchik, *Out of the Whirlwind: Essays on Mourning, Suffering, and the Human Condition*, ed. David Schatz, Joel B. Wolowelsky, and Reuven Ziegler (New York: Ktav, 2003), 206.

274 Abraham Maslow, *Toward a Psychology of Being* (New York: D. van Nostrand, 1968), 61.

275 Abraham Maslow, "Neurosis as a Failure of Personal Growth," *Humanitas* 3 (1967): 165–66.

CHAPTER 24

276 One Jewish articulation of this view is found in Maimonides's Ninth
Principle of Faith: "I believe with perfect faith that this Torah will
not be exchanged and there will be no other Torah from the Creator"
(https://www.sefaria.org.il/Siddur_Ashkenaz%2C_Weekday%2C_
Shacharit%2C_Post_Service%2C_Thirteen_Principles_of_Jewish_
Faith?lang=bi). For a Christian perspective on the issue, see "Chicago
Statement on Biblical Inerrancy," *Journal of the Evangelical Theological
Society* 21, no. 4 (December 1978): 289–96.

277 Rabbi Aharon Lichtenstein, "Torah and General Culture: Confluence
and Conflict," in *Judaism's Encounter with Other Cultures: Rejection or
Integration?*, ed. Jacob J. Schacter (Lanham, MD: Rowman & Little-
field, 1997), 226–27.

278 For more references of traditional commentators treating biblical
figures as flawed humans, see Nachmanides on Abraham's famine
(Genesis 12) and on Sarah's banishment of Hagar (Genesis 16); Rabbi
Samson Raphael Hirsch (on Genesis 12:10, 25:27; Exodus 6:14);
Rabbi Yitzchak Hutner (*Pachad Yitzchak, Igrot U'ketavim*, letter 128);
Joel Wolowelsky, "Kibbud Av and Kibbud Avot," *Tradition* 33, no. 4
(1999): 35–44; Hayyim Angel, "Learning Faith from the Text, or Text
from Faith," in *Wisdom from All My Teachers*, ed. Jeffrey Saks and Susan
Handelman (Jerusalem: Urim and ATID, 2003); A. David, "Perspec-
tives on the Avot and Imahot," *Ten Da'at* 5, no. 2 (1991); Z. Grumet,
"Another Perspective on the Avot and Imahot," *Ten Da'at* 6, no. 1
(1992); H. Dietcher, "Between Angels and Mere Mortals: Nechama
Leibowitz' Approach to the Study of Biblical Characters," *Journal of
Jewish Education* 66, no. 1–2 (2000).

279 Indeed, he was not permitted to build the Temple due to the blood on
his hands (I Chronicles 22:8), to name just one example.

280 *Vayikra Rabbah* 7:2.

281 Leonard Cohen, "Anthem," in *The Future* (Columbia Records, 1992).

CHAPTER 25

282 "Who is a God like You, forgiving inequity and remitting transgres-
sion; who has not maintained God's wrath forever against the rem-
nant of God's own people, because God loves graciousness! God will
take us back in love; God will cover our iniquities, You will hurl all our
sins into the depths of the sea. You will keep faith with Jacob, loyalty to
Abraham, as You promised on oath to our ancestors in days gone by."
(Micah 7:18–20)

283 Chaim Jachter, *Depths of Yonah: Unleashing the Power of Your Yom Kippur* (self-pub., 2018), 154; see https://www.blurb.com/b/8870724-depths-of-yonah).
284 *Yalkut Shimoni* 551.
285 Mother Teresa, *In the Heart of the World: Thoughts, Stories, and Prayers* (Novato, CA: New World Library, 1997).
286 *Pirkei D'Rabbi Eliezer* 10, *Yalkut* 551.
287 Abarbanel on Jonah 3:1 (based on the work *Seder Olam*, which he references).
288 See Krista Tippett, *Becoming Wise: An Inquiry into the Mystery and Art of Living* (New York: Penguin Press, 2016), 68.
289 Joseph Campbell, *Reflections on the Art of Living*, 18 [n201].
290 David Kimchi on Jonah 1:1.
291 Jonah's experience with the *kikayon* is the only place in the book where there is any indication of an experience of joy.
292 To be sure, it is not entirely strange to feel connected to a plant. After all, a tree (representing life) is one of the paradigmatic metaphors for the Torah: "She is a tree of life to those who grasp her, and whoever holds on to her is happy" (Proverbs 3:18).
293 Radak on Jonah 3:5; Ibn Ezra on Jonah 3:2.
294 Rashi on Jonah 1:5.
295 Like the *kikayon* withers without Jonah's compassion.
296 Susan Sontag, *Regarding the Pain of Others* (New York: Farrar, Straus and Giroux, 2003), 101.
297 Lawrence Kushner, *God Was in This Place and I, I Did Not Know: Finding Self, Spirituality, and Ultimate Meaning* (Woodstock, VT: Jewish Lights, 1991), 25.

CONCLUSION
298 *Zohar* on *Chayei Sarah*.
299 Klitsner, *Subversive Sequels in the Bible*, 29.

About the Author

RABBI DR. SHMULY YANKLOWITZ is the President and Dean of Valley Beit Midrash, Founder and President of Uri L'Tzedek, Founder and CEO of Shamayim, and Founder and President of YATOM: The Jewish Foster and Adoption Network.

Rabbi Yanklowitz's writings have appeared in outlets as diverse as the *New York Times*, *Wall Street Journal*, *Washington Post*, *Guardian*, and *Atlantic*. Rabbi Yanklowitz is a sought-after educator, social justice activist, and motivational speaker as well as the author of nineteen books on Jewish spirituality, social justice, and ethics.

Rabbi Yanklowitz has volunteered, staffed trips, and taught across the world, including in Israel, Ghana, India, France, Thailand, El Salvador, England, Senegal, Germany, Switzerland, Ukraine, Argentina, South Africa, and Haiti. Rabbi Yanklowitz has served as a rabbinic representative and speaker at the World Economic Forum in Geneva and Davos. His religious journey was filmed in the Independent Lens/PBS documentary *The Calling*.

Rabbi Yanklowitz earned a master's degree from Harvard University in Leadership and Psychology, another master's from Yeshiva University in Jewish Philosophy, and a doctorate from Columbia University in Moral Development and Epistemology. He obtained rabbinical ordination from the Yeshivat Chovevei Torah Rabbinical School and two private ordinations in Israel. He has twice been named one of America's Top Rabbis by *Newsweek*. In 2016, the *Forward* named Rabbi Yanklowitz one of the Most Inspiring Rabbis in America. The same year, the *Forward* named him one of the fifty most influential Jews.

Rabbi Yanklowitz, his wife Shoshana, and their four children live in Scottsdale, Arizona. They are also foster parents.

CPSIA information can be obtained
at www.ICGtesting.com
Printed in the USA
BVHW042057120820
586225BV00006B/52